# Separation and Creativity

# THE LACANIAN CLINICAL FIELD

*A series of books edited by*
*Judith Feher Gurewich, Ph.D.*
*in collaboration with Susan Fairfield*

# Separation and Creativity

REFINDING THE LOST LANGUAGE OF CHILDHOOD

Maud Mannoni

*Translated by*
*Susan Fairfield*

**OTHER**

Other Press
*New York*

Production Editor: Robert D. Hack

This book was set in 12 pt. New Baskerville by Alpha Graphics of Pittsfield, New Hampshire.

Copyright © 1999 by Other Press, Llc. Copyright © 1993 by Éditions DENÕEL.

10 9 8 7 6 5 4 3 2 1

**Library of Congress Cataloging-in-Publication Data**

Mannoni, Maud, 1923–
    [Amour, haine, séparation. English]
    Separation and creativity : refinding the lost language of
childhood / Maud Mannoni : translated by Susan Fairfield.
       p.  cm. — (The Lacanian clinical field)
    Includes bibliographical references and index.
    ISBN 1-892746-20-4 (pbk. : alk. paper)
    1. Psychoanalysis. 2. Separation (Psychology). 3. Autobiography.
I. Title. II. Series.
BF175.M265313  1999
150.19'5—dc21                   98-50475

*For Léa*

*Ny olombelona hoatra ny ladimboatavo; ka raha fotorana, iray ihany.* (The living are like the branchings of a pumpkin vine; at the base there is just a single branch.)

Proverb

# Contents

# The Lacanian Clinical Field: Series Overview

Lacanian psychoanalysis exists, and the new series, The Lacanian Clinical Field, is here to prove it. The clinical expertise of French practitioners deeply influenced by the thought of Jacques Lacan has finally found a publishing home in the United States. Books that have been acclaimed in France, Italy, Spain, Greece, South America, and Japan for their clarity, didactic power, and clinical relevance will now be at the disposal of the American psychotherapeutic and academic communities. These books cover a range of topics, including theoretical introductions; clinical approaches to neurosis, perversion, and psychosis; child psychoanalysis; conceptualizations of femininity; psychoanalytic readings of American literature; and more. Thus far nine books are in preparation.

Though all these works are clinically relevant, they will also be of great interest to those American scholars who have taught and used Lacan's theories for over a decade. What better opportunity for the academic world of literary criticism, philosophy, human sciences, women's studies, film studies, and multicultural studies finally to have access to the clinical insights of a theorist known primarily for his revolutionary vision of the formation of the human subject. Thus The Lacanian Clinical Field goes beyond introducing the American clinician to a different psychoanalytic outlook. It brings together two communities that have grown progressively estranged from each other. For indeed, the time when the Frankfurt School, Lionel Trilling, Erich Fromm, Herbert Marcuse, Philip Rieff, and others were fostering exchanges between the academic and the psychoanalytic communities is gone, and in the process psychoanalysis has lost some of its vibrancy.

The very limited success of ego psychology in bringing psychoanalysis into the domain of science has left psychoanalysis in need of a metapsychology that is able not only to withstand the pernicious challenges of psychopharmacology and psychiatry but also to accommodate the findings of cognitive and developmental psychology. Infant research has put many of Freud's insights into question, and the attempts to replace a one-body psychology with a more interpersonal or intersubjective approach have led to dissension within the psychoanalytic community. Many theorists are of the opinion that the road toward scientific legitimacy requires a certain allegiance with Freud's detractors, who are convinced that the unconscious and its sexual underpinnings are merely an aberration. Psychoanalysis continues to be practiced, however, and according to both patients and analysts the uncovering of unconscious motivations continues to provide a sense of relief. But while there has been a burgeoning of different psychoanalytic schools of thought since the desacralization of Freud, no theoretical agreement has been reached as to why such relief occurs.

Nowadays it can sometimes seem that Freud is read much more scrupulously by literary critics and social scientists than by psychoanalysts. This is not entirely a coincidence. While the psychoanalytic community is searching for a new metapsychology, the human sciences have acquired a level of theoretical sophistication and complexity that has enabled them to read Freud under a new lens. Structural linguistics and structural anthropology have transformed conventional appraisals of human subjectivity and have given Freud's unconscious a new status. Lacan's teachings, along with the works of Foucault and Derrida, have been largely responsible for the explosion of new ideas that have enhanced the interdisciplinary movement pervasive in academia today.

The downside of this remarkable intellectual revolution, as far as psychoanalysis is concerned, is the fact that Lacan's contribution has been derailed from its original trajectory. No longer perceived as a theory meant to enlighten the practice of psychoanalysis, his brilliant formulations have been both adapted and criticized so as to conform to the needs of purely intellectual endeavors far removed from clinical reality. This state of affairs is certainly in part responsible for Lacan's dismissal by the psychoanalytic community. Moreover, Lacan's "impossible" style has been seen as yet another proof of the culture of obscurantism that French intellectuals seem so fond of.

In this context the works included in The Lacanian Clinical Field should serve as an eye-opener at both ends of the spectrum. The authors in the series are primarily clinicans eager to offer to professionals in psychoanalysis, psychiatry, psychology, and other mental-health disciplines a clear and succinct didactic view of Lacan's work. Their goal is not so much to emphasize the radically new insights of the Lacanian theory of subjectivity and its place in the history of human sciences as it is to show how this difficult and complex body of ideas can enhance clinical work. Therefore, while the American clinician will be made aware that Lacanian psychoanalysis is not primarily a staple of literary criticism or philosophy but a praxis meant to cure patients of their psychic distress, the academic community will be exposed for the first time to a reading of Lacan that is in sharp contrast with the literature that has thus far informed them about his theory. In that sense Lacan's teachings return to the clinical reality to which they primarily belong.

Moreover, the clinical approach of the books in this series will shed a new light on the critical amendments that literary scholars and feminist theoreticians have brought to Lacan's conceptualization of subjectivity. While Lacan has been applauded for having offered an alternative to Freud's biological determinism, he has also been accused of nevertheless remaining phallocentric in his formulation of sexual difference. Yet this criticism, one that may be valid outside of the clinical reality—psychoanalysis is both an ingredient and an effect of culture—may not have the same relevance in the clinical context. For psychoanalysis as a praxis has a radically different function from the one it currently serves in academic discourse. In the latter, psychoanalysis is perceived both as an ideology fostering patriarchal beliefs and as a theoretical tool for constructing a vision of the subject no longer dependent on a phallocratic system. In the former, however, the issue of phallocracy loses its political impact. Psychoanalytic practice can only retroactively unravel the ways in which the patient's psychic life has been constituted, and in that sense it can only reveal the function the phallus plays in the psychic elaboration of sexual difference.

The Lacanian Clinical Field, therefore, aims to undo certain prejudices that have affected Lacan's reputation up to now in both the academic and the psychoanalytic communities. While these prejudices stem from rather different causes—Lacan is perceived as too patriarchal and reactionary in the one and too far removed from clinical reality in the other—they both seem to overlook the fact that the fifty years that cover the period of Lacan's teachings were mainly devoted to working and reworking the meaning and function of psychoanalysis, not necessarily as a science or even as a human science, but as a practice that can nonetheless rely on a solid and coherent metapsychology. This double debunking of received notions may not only enlarge the respective frames of reference of both the therapeutic and the academic communities; it may also allow them to find a common denominator in a metapsychology that has derived its "scientific" status from the unexpected realm of the humanities.

I would like to end this overview to the series as a whole with a word of warning and a word of reassurance. One of the great difficulties for an American analyst trying to figure out the Lacanian "genre" is the way these clinical theorists explain their theoretical point of view as if it were coming straight from Freud. Yet Lacan's Freud and the American Freud are far from being transparent to each other. Lacan dismantled the Freudian corpus and rebuilt it on entirely new foundations, so that the new edifice no longer resembled the old. At the same time he always downplayed, with a certain *coquetterie*, his position as a theory builder, because he was intent on proving that he had remained, despite all odds, true to Freud's deepest insights. Since Lacan was very insistent on keeping Freudian concepts as the raw material of his theory, Lacanian analysts of the second generation have followed in their master's footsteps and have continued to read Freud scrupulously in order to expand, with new insights, this large structure that had been laid out. Moreover, complicated historical circumstances have fostered their isolation, so that their acquaintance with recent psychoanalytic developments outside of France has been limited. Lacan's critical views on ego psychology and selected aspects of object relations theory have continued to inform their vision of American psychoanalysis and have left them unaware that certain of their misgivings about these schools of thought are shared by some of their colleagues in the United States. This apparently undying allegiance to Freud, therefore, does not necessarily mean that Lacanians have not moved beyond him, but rather that their approach is different from that of their American counterparts. While the latter often tend to situate their work as a reaction to Freud, the Lacanian strategy always consists in rescuing Freud's insights and resituating them in a context free of biological determinism.

Second, I want to repeat that the expository style of the books of this series bears no resemblance to Lacan's own writings. Lacan felt that Freud's clarity and didactic talent had ultimately led to distortions and oversimplifications, so that his own notoriously "impossible" style was meant to serve as a metaphor for the difficulty of listening to the unconscious. Cracking his difficult writings involves not only the intellectual effort of readers but also their unconscious processes; comprehension will dawn as reader-analysts recognize in their own work what was expressed in sibylline fashion in the text. Some of Lacan's followers continued this tradition, fearing that clear exposition would leave no room for the active participation of the reader. Others felt strongly that although Lacan's point was well taken it was not necessary to prolong indefinitely an ideology of obscurantism liable to fall into the same traps as the ones Lacan was denouncing in the first place. Such a conviction was precisely what made this series, The Lacanian Clinical Field, possible.

—Judith Feher Gurewich, Ph.D.

# Introduction

JOHN BRENKMAN

Before Prozac arrived to alter the moods of millions, Maud Mannoni thought to delve with her emotionally disturbed and learning-impaired young patients into the meaning of the sadness and terror in their existence. The play, art, and talk of therapy were a means for these children to express themselves from the place of their distress and fear. Before schools started dispensing Ritalin daily so that children, many of whom live in households beleaguered by poverty, emotional chaos, violence, or alcohol, will pay attention to the teacher, Mannoni dared to undertake psychoanalysis with backward children and their parents, exploring the links between learning disorders and the child's history within his or her family. How, she asked, does the child's speech disorder, reading and math problems, or disorientation in space and time connect to his or her inner psychic-body reality? And, conversely, what role does the child's "illness" or "deficiency" play for his or her parents and siblings, and how does that meaning rebound back on the child as the distorting mirror in which he or she struggles to sense who he or she is?

Reading *Separation and Creativity: Refinding the Lost Language of Childhood* stirs up a disturbing nostalgia. The boldness of Mannoni's therapeutic experiments, especially at Bonneuil, where she founded a residential treatment institution for emotionally disturbed children, replete with theater experiments guided by the avant-garde director Jerzy Grotowski and storytelling by an African griot, might seem a mere throwback to 1968. Until one asks: *Why* does it seem a throwback?

Over the past thirty years, psychiatry has steadily narrowed its scope, replacing psychotherapy with pharmacy prescriptions. Meanwhile, hundreds of therapies have bloomed within American culture, most of them guided by self-help prescriptions. Common wisdom has it that psychoanalysis has been rendered obsolete. I do not have the expertise to evaluate the validity or dangers of today's most widely used psycho-pharmaceutical treatments, and certainly do not question the reality of clinical depression, but it is startlingly clear that the medical faith in benign smack and the social worker pill simply sets aside the notion that human beings have something to learn from the meaning of their terror or distraction, and that the transformation of their relation to themselves and others might require giving expression to that meaning. Can genetics, neurophysiology, and pharmacology really explain the psychosomatic complexity of human beings by bypassing the kind of self-questioning and dialogue that are the hallmark of Mannoni's psychoanalytic procedure?

That is the question one hopes the publication, in English, of *Separation and Creativity* might prompt American psychoanalysts, psychiatrists, and psychologists to seriously entertain. At issue is not how psychoanalysis might duel for prestige with popular treatments, but rather how it might rethink and actively pursue its relation to them.

I recently heard the French psychoanalyst Michel Tort make a penetrating, thoughtful criticism of the efforts that a young Lacanian analyst in the United States is making in treating children diagnosed with hyperactivity and attention deficit disorder (ADD). The analyst is genuinely alarmed at the tendency to treat these children with Ritalin instead of psychotherapy; she sees in this an externalization of the children's disorders at the expense of fostering their capacity to articulate their distress and desire. Her presentation brought to light many common motifs she has discovered in her patients' lives within their families and the bearing of that experience on their learning and behavioral problems. Tort, with great sympathy for the position she finds herself in, argued that it was a mistake to put the medical (or medicalized) approach to ADD and the psychoanalytic approach on the same plane, as though the analyst's task were to make psychotherapy replace Ritalin or provide an analytic interpretation of ADD to rival the medical interpretation.

Such an approach, Tort suggested, runs two risks. On the one hand, it unrealistically flies in the face of the simple fact that doctors and teachers will inevitably treat ADD with drugs and specialized education; on the other hand, and more significantly, in looking to replace the medical and educational approach, whether conceptually or in practice, the analyst in effect accepts the medical definition of what the disorder is. Tort suggested that, instead, the analyst must first preserve the specificity of psychoanalysis and recognize that its work must proceed at an oblique angle to the medical approach. Each case has to be analyzed on whatever terms the analyst can find, pulling on whatever threads of the child's history and unconscious the analysis discloses. And, second, the analyst needs to make the medicalization of the child's problems itself an object of analysis: what can the child discover in the analytic dialogue about what it means, within his or her own psychic reality, to be in the eyes of others the bearer of a "symptom," "illness," or "deficiency" and to be "treated" with a mood-altering drug? The power of psychoanalysis lies in its specificity and even its limits. Its task is to expand the area of experience that can be articulated in the individual's own terms and own name, and therefore must leave open, case by case, how that project will mesh or not with the medical and educational goal of normalizing the child's behavior.

Confronting the uneasy relationship between psychoanalysis and the social aims of psychiatric and educational institutions was Maud Mannoni's life work. In the school she founded at Bonneuil in 1969, the aims of psychotherapy were kept significantly separate from the other, no less essential needs of the patients. The art and theater studios were a protected space of creativity, supervised by the analysts and trainees, while the kitchen was the space in which the children could welcome "guests from the outside." The "outside" world was also addressed through exchanges with other schools in letters, paintings, and a school paper, and the children had contact with "a variety of host families, artisans, and peasants in the area of Bonneuil." Most significantly perhaps, the staff did not participate in the children's schooling, which was carried out in correspondence courses: "In this way, the teacher who corrects and annotates their work is 'elsewhere,' and the adults at Bonneuil are there as companions to ease the enormous difficulties some of these children have."

Life in the school revolved around two kinds of activities. On the one hand, the children participated through the morning Chat Time and other meetings in discussing rules and voicing complaints, managing the food budget, and regulating their own life together within the facility. And, on the other, the studios provided a secure space for the children's creative activities: "we had to ensure the existence of a permanent frame within which free creative expression could take place, a frame that reflects the way human beings deal with aggressivity. If the frame is not maintained, the patient finds himself alone in his fantasy world, and when he suddenly loses the container for his anxiety, he acts out. . . . In each studio, the session opened with a mythic ritual serving to bring the children together. What they did after that was up to them. Speech can arise from a field of language, but not from a cacophony."

The separation of the protected space of creative expression from the disciplined space of schooling, of psychotherapy from dealings with the "outside" world, of the children's provisional life together within the institution from their social responsibilities in the community or at work, reflects Mannoni's attentiveness to the two sides of her patients' painful ordeal. On the one hand, they must find the means of expressing even their most stifled or destructive impulses, their most anti-social urges or most private fears, in an increasingly articulate form, that is, as an expression of themselves that can be shared with others without the risk of destroying the self or the other; and, on the other hand, they must develop their capacity to deal with real-world obligations and dangers without being defeated by the outside world's perception of them as ill or retarded.

The dynamics of this Scylla and Charybdis of children's psychotherapy is evident in Bonneuil's approach to art. Painting "made possible the expression, the projection (on paper placed on the floor or pinned onto the wall), of latent disorder, dormant conflicts, all the vio-

lence and hate held in and unusable in real life but waiting to burst forth on an Other stage, freeing the unconscious. Of course . . . this never proceeds smoothly. For
there are many symptoms that have to be integrated into
the painting by finding the right words that will enable
the child to displace a crisis."

And with the autistic children, for whom painting
was often their only means of expression, the risks of
expression could be so extreme they literally could not
hold a paint brush in their hands:

> One day we said to François, "That's because your
> mother puts you in her hands so that you won't have
> hands anymore." He began to shout and to weep,
> and then he painted the horror that was inside him.
> These horrors that could not be put into words al-
> ways seemed to involve unthinkable separation anxi-
> ety. When every separation is experienced as anni-
> hilation, all the child can do is construct for himself
> a world in which he tries hard to live without affects
> in order to keep himself safe from the threat of de-
> struction. When, thanks to analysis, he loses his au-
> tistic armor, he still has far to go: having become
> vulnerable, he remains fascinated by death and runs
> the risk of suicidal acting out.

One innovation at Bonneuil, apparently tried out without the staff forseeing the results, was to have the children, after each session, place their paintings on a huge

sheet of paper on the wall called the "tree of life." Then, "at the end of the year, the children selected which pictures they wanted to be shown in the gallery of paintings and which were to be burned 'to feed the earth.'" To the therapists' surprise and enlightenment, the children typically destroyed the paintings that were most interesting and revealing "from the analytical point of view." It was their way of regulating how they themselves would be seen by the world outside the studio of self-expression: "They were hardly concerned with the pictures to be exhibited, but what *had to be* destroyed seemed crucial to them, enabling them to survive as subjects and not be reduced to manipulated objects. This destruction represented the erasure of their shame, their fear, their fear of being labeled, yet again, as crazy."

In this wonderful anecdote Mannoni shows the fraught process through which her patients parried the risky expression of self as they let their unconscious speak in their paintings and the equally risky exposure of themselves to a social world perhaps not ready to hear them without pathologizing them. Between the "Other scene" of the unconscious and the social scene of judgmental others, the children found an intermediary space, the "sacrificial 'ceremony' in which [they] danced and sang around the fire" watching their paintings burn.

Reading these essays by Mannoni left me flush with a nostalgia of my own. I first came across her work in 1977 when I happened on a copy of *The Backward Child and His Mother* while visiting New York City; it was being remaindered at the Barnes and Noble Annex on 18th Street for a dollar. Reading it on the plane home was an intellectual epiphany. She created a bridge between the two developments in post-Freudian theory that I found most compelling and yet irreconcilable: the work of Jacques Lacan and of the British anti-psychiatrists R. D. Laing and David Cooper. A further dimension of Mannoni's dialogue with British psychoanalysis is evident in the essays collected in *Separation and Creativity*, where she fruitfully connects many of the insights and perspectives of D. W. Winnicott to Lacanian theory.

Mannoni took psychoanalysis into the psychiatric setting of mental institutions, entering and challenging the very space in which society isolates and labels the mad and the retarded. At the same time, she used the Lacanian emphasis on the role of language and speaking in the formation of the "subject" and in the dynamics of the therapeutic dialogue to shed new light on the Laingian themes of the politics of the family and the role of others in shaping, thwarting, and distorting the "self."

Along with her husband Octave Mannoni and Fançoise Dolto, Maud Mannoni belonged to the first generation of Lacan's disciples, already trained and practicing analysis long before Lacan's seminars went public in 1964 when he delivered *Seminar XI: The Four Fundamental Concepts of Psychoanalysis* to a burgeoning audience of students at the École normale supérieure. For anyone outside the Parisian psychoanalytic scene, the therapy subculture of Lacanianism of the late 60s and early 70s,

trying to picture what Lacanian analysis was all about as
a therapeutic technique took a strange labor of conjec-
ture and surmise, since Lacan himself presented no case
histories in his *Écrits* or in the Seminars that dribbled to
America in mimeographed summaries and eventually in
published form. The precise nature of what he repeat-
edly alludes to as the "analytic experience" had to be
guessed at, essentially by trying to reimagine Freud's five
case histories in Lacan's theoretical terms.

*The Backward Child and His Mother* provided the miss-
ing link. The defining feature of Lacanian therapy lies
in its attention to the formative role of the desires and
demands of "the Other"—principally, the mother and
father—in shaping the desire, identity, and symptoms of
the "subject." According to Lacanian theory, this inter-
.subjective formation of the "subject" ultimately stems
from language, since language is the structuring medium
of human intersubjectivity in general. Even the "pre-
verbal" interactions of mother and child are viewed by
Lacan as linguistically mediated interactions: the baby's
needs are answered by the mother as a "request for love"
(*demande d'amour*), so that even the child's most inarticu-
late cries come back to it from the mother as a discursively
significant utterance; the infant (*in-fans* = speechless) has
conveyed to him or her the "symbolic" markers of filiation and gender, that is, the names and codes of family
and sexual identity; and the primary processes of the
unconscious (displacement and condensation in Freud's
idiom, metonymy and metaphor in Lacan's) work accord-

ing to the rules of linguistic articulation. In turn, Lacanians view the analytic dialogue or "talking cure" not merely as the occasion for verbalization but as a site of inter-subjectivity that arises from, and is inextricably bound to, the linguistically mediated history and unconscious of the subject.

Mannoni's work foregrounds the ways in which the mother's fantasy and history are inscribed in the emotionally troubled child's symptoms, body image, and capacities for verbal and artistic expression. Her clinical attentiveness to the child's struggle to articulate his or her desire and fear in a language freed from the saturating symbols of the parents' fears and desires shows how empty talk (*parole vide*) becomes full speaking (*parole pleine*) in a way one could only faintly deduce from Lacan's tantalizing theorems about the dialectic of the "analytic experience." The vital heritage of Mannoni's clinical innovations has come to fruition most recently in, for example, the startling and bold work of Catherine Mathelin, whose *Lacanian Psychotherapy with Children: The Broken Piano* (Other Press, 1999) has recently appeared in English.

But Mannoni's work had little or no impact among the literary critics and cultural theorists who created the American context for discussions of Lacanian theory. The barrier perhaps to an adequate reception of Mannoni in the poststructuralist moment lay in the most striking feature of her work: its humanism. The French philosophical scene dominated by Althusser, Derrida, and Foucault used a rhetoric of anti-humanism to attack the notion of

upper-case Man, whether as the universal subject of history, image of God, or vessel of a promised overcoming
of alienation. Lacan's own very Cartesian anti-Cartesian
idiom resonated with this anti-humanism; he reveled in
the slogan that Freud's discovery of the unconscious was
a second Copernican revolution, displacing Man's ego
from the center of the universe. But the early Lacanian
analysts like Mannoni and Dolto hewed to a lower-case
humanism in their innovative therapeutic experiments.

The predicaments of the psychotic or neurotic child
are, for Mannoni, variations of the predicaments of
human existence and all human relations. Like Melanie
Klein, Laing, and Winnicott, she sees a genuine experience of madness in the most universal and normal childhood experiences: the terror of abandonment or dread
of annihilation, the ecstacy of omnipotence or thrill of
dependence, the impulse to murder or fear of destroying a loved one. And, conversely, she sees in children's
games, fantasies, and imaginings, even in their symptoms,
the origins and patterns of human creativity in general,
whether in life or art. Several of the essays collected here
reflect on creativity in literature and art. While Mannoni's
commentaries on Edith Wharton, Edgar Allan Poe, and
Pirandello are largely derivative from other psychoanalytic critics (and, like them, tend to ignore the formal
imperatives of literary creation), she does make sugges-
tive links between her own extraordinary exploration of
children's artistic creativity and receptivity and the significance of literary creativity in general. The essays are a

reminder that this important link between psychoanalysis and criticism has remained strangely fallow in the last two decades of Lacan's influence on literary criticism and theory.

The vivid sense that the disorders of troubled children and the conditions of the human soul lie on a single continuum informs all of Mannoni's work, whether she is discussing psychotic children, the response to historical trauma by survivors of the Holocaust, or the creative process of writers and artists. At Bonneuil she and her staff continually addressed themselves to the anxieties provoked *within themselves* by working and communicating with the disturbed children they treated.

Mannoni's humanism also shows in the value she gives to autonomy. Lacan's important polemic against American "ego psychology" and its suppositions of an integral, adaptive self's mastery over the unconscious and his stance against Cartesian and Husserlian conceptions of the certitude of the *cogito* inflected his theoretical vocabulary with some of its most charged, productive terms: the division of the subject, the subjection of the subject to the signifier, the unconscious as the discourse of the Other, and so on. Mannoni's work, in bringing to light the therapeutic stakes of the subject's formation in the discourse of the Other, gives these Lacanian concepts a different stress. She encountered children who could not learn to read and write because their deficiency itself satisfied in their mother a need to suffer in caring for a debilitated child; children who could not master their bodily movements because they were afraid that their mobility, and hence their independence, would cause their mother to die; children who could not recognize their own father in a strange setting because he did not acknowledge their presence at home; children who could not speak in the first person because language for them was clotted by the demands and labels others always articulated for them. For such children, "autonomy" is not an ideologically suspect mystification, it is an ordeal they must go through and a capacity they must acquire.

The Lacanian insight remains intact in Mannoni. Autonomy is not a given or even a settled achievement of the individual. The mastery of the image and movements of one's body (the imaginary dimension of autonomy) and the capacity to participate on a par with others in communication (the symbolic dimension of autonomy) are contradictory processes in which the desires and demands of others are always in play. At one point Mannoni refers to what Winnicott calls "the perpetual human task of keeping inner and outer reality separate yet inter-related." Again the note of humanism: the most elemental ordeals of the disturbed child are at the same time the ongoing challenge of human experience. Just as the differentiation of inside and outside is perpetual, the task of locating oneself in relation to one's "own" hidden desires in order to act upon them or not and the task of separating oneself from the demands or desires of another in order to respond to them or not are the always unfinished ordeal of human autonomy.

The Lacanian "I" is dynamic, divided, enmeshed and active within the intersubjectivity of langauge and desire, in a way that the Cartesian *cogito* or ego psychology's "self" is not. From discourse theory, one might also cite Mikhail Bakhtin to get at this dialectical conception of the intersubjective conditions of autonomy: "language, for the individual consciousness, lies on the borderline between oneself and the other. The word in language is half someone else's. It becomes 'one's own' only when the speaker populates it with his own intention, his own accent, when he appropriates the word, adapting it to his own semantic and expressive intention. Prior to this moment of appropriation, the word does not exist in a neutral and impersonal language (it is not, after all, out of a dictionary that the speaker gets his words!), but rather it exists in other people's mouths, in other people's contexts, serving other people's intentions: it is from there that one must take the word, and make it one's own." *And make it one's own.* Nowhere are the stakes and drama of this discovery of one's own intentions and accents and desire in the field of the other more vividly in evidence that in the studios of Bonneuil and in the mouths and hands of Mannoni's psychotic, retarded, and autistic young patients.

# 1

## Trauma and Creation

In his *Autobiographical Study*, Freud (1925) speaks of "the realm of the imagination" as "a 'reservation' made during the painful transition from the pleasure principle to the reality principle in order to provide a substitute for instinctual satisfaction which had to be given up in real life" (p. 64). He thereby admits that it is possible, through recreation, to escape the constraints of reality. But he does not name the place in which cultural experience is to be located, although, as early as 1908, he had written that

> every child at play becomes like a creative writer, in that he creates a world of his own, or, rather, rearranges the things of his world in a new way which pleases him. It would be wrong to think he does not take that world seriously; on the contrary, he takes

his play very seriously and he expends large amounts of emotion on it. The opposite of play is not what is serious but what is real. [1908a, p. 145]

Winnicott (1971) deserves credit for deepening this notion of cultural experience by discerning, alongside psychic reality and external reality, a third place, called *potential space*, located between the individual and the environment. This play space is, for him, the condition of the truth of the subject. As Octave Mannoni (1980) writes, "If there is no play and no maternal counter-play, the transition from dependence to independence is impaired" (p. 126). In such a case, the child forms a defensive armor and is at risk of developing into an echo of the mother's false self.

Winnicott emphasizes the importance of this stage of life in which the capacity for creativity is acquired or lost. He associates health with hopefulness, suffering, and a creative possibility that can transform pain into joy. For this to happen, the subject must not remain a captive of his daydreams or of a trauma that he has experienced, and he must have an imaginary public to whom he can speak without remaining imprisoned in a relation to others—that is, to himself, caught up in the net of his fantasy (cf. O. Mannoni 1988).

When the child suddenly finds himself unable to count on those around him, his play space becomes impoverished. As Winnicott (1971) observes, once the child does not feel safe enough to take pleasure in life, it is no longer possible for him to transcend a loss by using separation to express pleasure. Where Freud thinks in terms of psychic reality and instinctual vicissitudes (cf. M. Mannoni 1979), Winnicott speaks of a search for the self, with the attendant risk of self-loss. In emphasizing the fact that the child creates the object (the breast) that he can refind later on, Winnicott shows the crucial significance of this phase in which the child loses the feeling of omnipotence (a loss that cannot occur without the experience of aggressivity), and he notes the importance of the symbolization produced by these initial mechanisms of creation and imagination. As Françoise Dolto (1981) has said, the child, at first, does not *have* the object; he *is* it: the lost object is the self. It is only after the mirror stage[1] that the subject becomes a "me for you," a "me with you." It now becomes possible to divide up "having," so that the child can *have* the breast on the assumption that he *is not* it.

The ability to overcome the traumas of childhood (bereavements, separations, aggressions, among others) by achieving freedom through creation is not given to everyone. To overcome trauma in a production that may have artistic value is to re-create the initial experience of

---

1. In his study of "The mirror stage as formative of the function of the I" (1949), Lacan speaks of the "crossroads" that introduces the child to human desire. This is the child's confrontation, at around six months, with his mirror image, and his great joy at recognizing himself as distinct from the other.

distress, and there are people who, despite their genius, never manage to produce anything or to free themselves from what was, for them, destructive early on. Still others remain prisoners of the trauma, brooding over it monotonously. Because there is no place left for fantasy,[2] the fantastic (O. Mannoni 1969, p. 98) breaks through: there is no Other stage on which play can unfold. For such patients, it is as though their activity were cut off from life. As Winnicott observes, they have sought shelter in an internal model set in place in earliest childhood, a shelter within which there is a world of omnipotence that does not refer to any reality.

How can the horrors, the distress, experienced in childhood constitute the very material of a work of art? I shall be asking this question by discussing the impasse in which some people, dedicated to repetition, remain outside the field of artistic invention, while others are able to free themselves through aesthetic creation (cf. Terr 1987).

As we know, Edgar Allan Poe, the second son of impoverished actors, had a difficult childhood. Abandoned by his father at the age of eighteen months, he was raised on the farm of his paternal grandparents before going on tour with his mother. Shortly after his father left,

---

2. By *fantasy* I mean both unconscious fantasy as well as daydreaming. Freud uses the word *Phantasie* to designate fantasy, and *Phantasieren* for the creative activity that sets it in motion (see Laplanche and Pontalis 1973, pp. 314–319).

a mentally retarded girl was born, whose paternity remained uncertain. It was only by chance that Edgar learned of his father's death from tuberculosis, and that he had an older brother who died at the age of twenty. When his mother moved to Boston and then to New York, friends had to send her food and clothing; indeed, her financial situation was so precarious that a plea for help was published in the *Richmond Enquirer* (cf. Bonaparte 1949). When the actress finally died in 1911, Edgar was alone in the house with his sister. His mother left him a miniature depicting the two of them, mother and son, and, as Lenore Terr (1987) points out, the sparkle in Mrs. Poe's eyes as she looks at her three-year-old son was to dominate the future work of Edgar Allan Poe.

The traumatic imprint on his childhood came from the loneliness he experienced, for hours on end, in the face of this death. In his distress, he could find no words to name the unnamable. It was not until the following day that a friend of his mother's, learning of the situation, took Edgar in and became a kind of adoptive mother to him. When he was scarcely out of adolescence, he married his cousin, a frail girl of thirteen, who, like Edgar's mother, eventually died of tuberculosis.

Poe's work (1941, 1971) is dominated by a fascination with death—real death, but with a basis in the fantastic. Beneath the horrible features of exposed corpses, the eyes of his mother continue to haunt him and, through him, the reader. Far from resting in peace, these corpses rise up terrifyingly, as though imbued with a re-

ality coming from without, incapable of being symbolized:
blood covers their bodies and comes out of their mouths
("The Mystery of Marie Roget"), the funerary chamber
stretches out into infinity ("Loss of Breath").

Death continued to accompany Poe's life. As an
adolescent, he had a hallucination of an icy hand touching his face, and his nights were haunted by frightening dreams in which women dressed in white, as if ris-
ing from a tomb, came toward him. Shortly before his
death these female figures haunted him in broad day-
light. Poe lived in a constant state of helplessness, unable to accept any sort of aid—born, as he told a friend,
to suffer. And, in fact, he sought death in opium and
alcohol (which eventually killed him), but the figure of
death was fundamentally necessary for him, inseparable
from art and beauty: "I could not love except where
Death/Was mingling his with Beauty's breath" (cited in
Bonaparte 1949, p. 61).

Yet not all of Poe's heroines are sublime in death.
Some die suffocated in a chimney ("The Murders in the
Rue Morgue"); others, strangled, float in the Seine ("The
Mystery of Marie Roget") or fall victim to various calami-
ties. In his insistence on showing death in the least expected guises, Poe is, as it were, seeking an audience that
will grant him a much-needed catharsis as he transposes
into fiction the terrors of his daily life. What he presents
is like pure theater: the reader participates in the most
primal emotions, identifying with the horror of the

author's experience. Although one and the same fantasy obsessed Poe throughout his life, his literary work liberated his daydreams and freed him up in another way (cf. O. Mannoni 1988, pp. 43–54). Poe continued to repeat the work of mourning, of death, of the unnamable, so as to give birth to the gift of a work separate from himself. But this creation, liberated though it was, remained captive to his imaginary relation to others, that is, to himself. He needed the masquerade that refers to the darkness persisting in all of us, and, through his imaginary readers, he obtained pardon for his crimes, even if the crime was only that of existing. *who is his Other?*

Edith Wharton, too, speaks urgently of loneliness, anguish, and alienation in her *Ghost Stories* (1973). Between the lines, in a mixture of the familiar and the strange, we discern the memory of her illness, typhoid fever: she was eight years old when an army doctor told her parents, in her presence, that she was going to die. She owed her survival to the merest chance, when the personal physician of the Czar of Russia, who happened to be passing through Mildbad, where she was staying, agreed to see the little girl. He changed her treatment and saved her, but at the price of being in total isolation in a wing of the hotel, where she had to remain for months. Her parents, fearing contagion, seldom came to see her, and her only visitor from the outside world was a doctor, masked and dressed in white. A nurse stayed in a nearby room, forbidden to leave the hotel (Terr 1987).

Thus the only person who spoke with the little girl every day—briefly—and discussed her condition with her parents was this doctor who looked like a ghost.

Once she left isolation and was convalescing, friends gave her "cops and robbers" stories to read. Edith gradually began to live in a state of vague fear that became chronic, her every step accompanied by a sense of threat. Soon she was unable to go to sleep without a nurse at her bedside. Returning from her daily walks, she was overcome by terror of what might spring out from behind the door and by a feeling of complete vulnerability. For eight years she lived with visual and auditory hallucinations. The traces of the illness persisted for a long time; at the age of twenty-seven she was still unable to fall asleep if there was a book of ghost stories in the room. She burned many such books, but, curiously, was cured only when she began to write her own ghost stories based on a forgotten historical truth.

If the delusional construct can be an attempt at healing, the transposition of trauma onto an Other stage through writing can have a liberating effect. The external threat thus becomes the reflection of a threatened internal world; the writer perceives a part of himself as if it concerned someone else, and time is canceled out to the point where it merges with space. The feeling of strangeness no longer arises once the boundaries between fantasy and reality are unclear and we enter the domain of fiction. As Wharton says in the Autobiographical Postscript to her *Ghost Stories*, the writer himself should be scared by the ghost stories he writes, so that he can succeed in communicating to the reader the feeling of strangeness that this type of story evokes, the effect of which is to abolish all distance between "health" and "madness."

In 1902 she wrote "The Lady's maid's bell," shortly before a so-called "neurasthenic" episode that appeared when she was around thirty-three. Nausea, fatigue, and weight loss repeated the symptoms of her typhoid fever, and the story begins with the words, "It was the autumn after I had the typhoid" (Wharton 1973, p. 6). The heroine, Hartley, a convalescent, is seeking employment as a lady's companion. She has been given the name of Mrs. Brympton, a semi-invalid, who lives in a large house with many servants, where Emma Saxon, the head servant, had passed away during the past spring. The husband is away most of the time; their two children are deceased. As she gets to know the lady who will be her employer, the girl gradually becomes aware of the oddness of the place. Her room, some distance away from Mrs. Brympton's, is opposite an empty room that must always remain closed off. The door was open when the girl took possession of her own room, and she learned from one of the servants that the condemned room had belonged to the dead woman. The unexpected arrival of Mr. Brympton disquiets her; he strikes her as gruff and coarse.

Sent into town by her employer to do some shopping, the girl meets an old acquaintance who seems frightened to hear that she has accepted this position and predicts that she will not last three months. Upon her return, Hartley hears her mistress being spoken to harshly by the husband, and it is then that she begins to feel that there is something strange in this house. She hears footsteps; she believes that her mistress is ringing for her, but it is just a dream. She passes in terror before the door of the empty room that is supposed to remain closed.

Once Mr. Brympton leaves, Hartley surveys the long corridor and sees, in the doorway of the forbidden room, Emma Saxon, who then leaves the house. Hartley has the impression of having let Emma Saxon disappear without having known what she wanted. It is hard for her to tell what is fantasy and what is reality: Did she or didn't she see Emma Saxon's ghost? When she returns to her room, terrified, she once again sees the vision of Emma Saxon emerging from the darkness and immediately vanishing. The bell rings, and Hartley hastens to her mistress, only to be told that she must have been dreaming. Footsteps are heard: Mr. Brympton is back. Hartley informs her mistress, who falls down dead.

In "The 'uncanny,'" Freud (1919) explains how, under the effect of repression, a feeling can be transformed into anxiety. This anxiety comes from the reappearance of the repressed element and is encountered in the form of uncanniness. He adds that fiction can create new forms of this feeling of uncanniness, ones that do not exist in real life, since it is in the nature of the imagination to do without confirmation by reality. Is this reality material or psychic? The question haunted Freud throughout his life.

The subject matter of "The Lady's maid's bell"— written just before the 33-year-old author, in a state of depression, was about to re-experience in her body the symptoms of the typhoid fever she had contracted at the age of eight—has its origin in childhood, in the trauma accompanying Wharton's isolation during her illness. Beyond the figure of the ghost, this tale is a staging of *forbidden curiosity*. The shape of Emma Saxon appears to Hartley only after she wondered whether the door of the empty room was open or shut. The feeling of strangeness that comes over her is produced by both discovery and recognition. It is connected with a forbidden knowledge, legible between the lines of this story and going back to a confusion not just between external reality and psychic reality but, once again, between health and madness.

In "Afterwards" (Wharton 1973), Wharton returns to the distress into which she had been plunged by the loneliness and the deception imposed on her by her illness. The isolation had seemed unbearable because it was not backed by a truthful account; the child was left without explanations, cut off day after day from the world of the living. The heroine of this story, Mary Boyne, likewise lives in a haunted house, terrified to the point where she loses her sense of time and feels like a piece of furniture that is being pushed around. The tone of the narrative reflects extreme anguish: the house somehow "knows" what is happening, and from this knowledge the heroine is excluded.

The themes of isolation and illness, and the uncanniness of the double (Freud 1919), also appear in "The triumph of night" (Wharton 1973). Freud dates the emergence of the double to the archaic period of psychic development. An image, originally benign, is later transformed into an image of horror; the distraught subject loses his bearings and can no longer clearly distinguish between himself and the external world. This story is one that Wharton originally wrote at the age of twelve and then again at fifteen. In the earlier version, the hero fell ill with pneumonia after a ball (cf. Terr 1987) and went to Nice to die. Thirty-five years later, Edith Wharton wrote "The triumph of the night," the story of a young man with tuberculosis, who is sent into isolation on the advice of his doctor and attempts to survive a diagnosis that condemns him. He does not feel ill but is aware of having become the instrument of a sentence that leaves him with no choice but to remain shut up in New Hampshire. The feeling of strangeness that he experiences comes from the revelation of what should have remained concealed from him. In this story, the notion of medical error probably involves a very primitive experience of a loss of confidence in adults who placed the author in danger.

In the quasi-autobiographical story "Mr. Jones" (Wharton 1973), an invisible phantom prevents entry to a young woman's home. Lady Jane, taking possession of the house she has inherited, learns from a servant, Mrs.

Clemm, that thirty years earlier Mr. Jones (the phantom) had left someone outside. Mrs. Clemm goes on to speak of the past of this house that is desperately empty though filled with servants. Lady Jane has a strange feeling on the doorstep, and then, walking through the deserted rooms, she comes upon a letter written by a young woman, on her deathbed, to her husband. This young woman complains about the medical care she has received and the seclusion in which she has been obliged to live. But did Mrs. Clemm have the right to hand over these papers? Hasn't she betrayed an inviolable secret? This is the question Lady Jane asks herself as, several days later, she finds Mrs. Clemm dead, strangled, her eyes open, her hand still warm. Lady Jane asks a little girl who is in the room where Mr. Jones is to be found. The child answers that he has been dead and buried for many years, and, terrified, goes on to say before falling in a faint that Lady Jane should not have looked at the papers, since this was what Mrs. Clemm had been punished for. This, she seems to be saying, is what happens when forbidden knowledge is sought.

It happens that Clemm is the maiden name of Edgar Allan Poe's wife, the daughter of his aunt Mrs. William Clemm (Terr 1987). This suggests that Wharton may have been trying to evoke her own life through the fascination with death that is so characteristic of the work of the earlier writer, whose existence was one long succession of post-traumatic repetitions.

According to Freud (1919), the distress accompany-

ing the feeling of uncanniness recalls the repetition compulsion; it is something that emerges from the shadows
in which it should have remained. What arouses anxiety,
then, is the return of the repressed. At certain times Edith
Wharton's stories take place in the domain of omnipotent thoughts and desires; she even speaks of the return
of the dead. Strangeness emanates over and over again
from solitude, silence, darkness—elements associated
with infantile anxiety. Yet fiction enables the author to
encompass both what is repressed and what has been
overcome.

The emergence of the fantastic awakens the super-
stition that lies dormant in all of us. Thus "All souls"
(Wharton 1973) is the story of an old woman, bedridden
with a sprained ankle and forbidden by her doctor to
walk. Mrs. Clayburn, seized with pain during the night,
rings and calls desperately for assistance. The electricity
is cut off; no one comes. The old woman gets up and, with
the help of her cane, walks through the house in the
darkness. She reaches the servants' room, but none of
them responds. It is beginning to grow cold, and Mrs.
Clayburn is trying to return to her room when she hears
a noise. Frozen with terror, she drops her cane and falls
in a faint. When she regains consciousness, she carefully
takes her husband's revolver, loads it, and locks herself
in her room.

Three days later, the servants return and call the
doctor, who is annoyed because his patient had gotten
out of bed. When one of the servants says that Mrs.

Clayburn should have rung for her, the old lady angrily denounces the lie and relates the horror of being left alone for three days with no electricity, telephone, or heat; she had to fire up the heat herself, she says, because the house was as cold as a tomb. Still in shock when a cousin comes to see her later on, she speaks of her distress and says that she will never come to this house again once she is cured.

Wharton wrote this story shortly before her death. She was thus strong enough to evoke, by way of transposition, the trauma that she herself had undergone at the age of eight, thereby enabling the reader to share in the anguish, the helplessness, of those who live in a world in which the only law is the arbitrariness of women and ghosts.

Freud wondered whether the representation of suffering could be a source of pleasure (cf. O. Mannoni 1968), and this led him to examine the compulsion to repeat unpleasant situations that we see, for example, in post-traumatic neurosis and in children's play. The repetition serves to transpose the disturbing event onto an Other stage, one that welcomes fantasy and dreaming. The artist, as he says,

> like the neurotic, had withdrawn from an unsatisfactory reality into this world of imagination; but, unlike the neurotic, he knew how to find a way back from it and once more to get a firm foothold in reality. His creations, works of art, were the imaginary

satisfactions of unconscious wishes, just as dreams are. [1925, pp. 64–65]

But they are created so that others may take part in them. The creator of literature, Freud (1919) tells us elsewhere, brings the reader an extra yield of pleasure and seduction that relaxes tension and permits the indulgence of fantasy. Childhood memories are very often visual (Freud 1901; cf. 1899), and, Freud tells us, are preserved like scenes from a play. What one finds are not so much the traces of real events as the traces of their subsequent elaborations. Childhood memories often take the form of screen memories similar to the recollections of the infancy of the human race as represented in myths and legends.

Alfred Hitchcock was, like Wharton, an admirer of Poe, and it was because of the fascination with Poe's stories that he created his suspense films. At a press conference in Hollywood in 1979, he spoke of the trauma that he experienced at the age of six (see Terr 1987). He had misbehaved, and his father, intending to punish the child and make an impression on him, took him to the local police station, explaining his intention in a written note he handed to the officer. The officer locked up the child for five minutes, saying, "That's what happens to bad boys." Ever since then, Hitchcock continued, he had always rebelled against any arrest and imprisonment. This "punitive expedition," though apparently innocent, remained engraved on his conscious memory.

Fearful of imprisonment and authority figures throughout adolescence, when Hitchcock became an adult he
found in his childhood experience the source for his
suspense films, transposing his fear by developing the
themes of injustice and the manhunt and passing his
anxiety onto the spectator: the police pursue a man for
a crime he didn't commit, an innocent man is killed by
the chief of police, a priest tries to win the acquittal of
a man for a murder for which someone else has admit-
ted responsibility during confession. Many of his films
make use of a similar theme: men or women unjustly
incarcerated.

Terr (1987) emphasizes some striking effects achieved
by various camera angles. For example, a prison is shot
from above in such a way as to make the adult character,
a man wrongly accused of sex murders, seem to be a
5-year-old child, desperate and lost, wandering in his cell.
Throughout his film-making career, Hitchcock needed
to focus the spectator's gaze on the horror of the imprisonment he himself had had to undergo as a child: his
creativity brings inner experience into the realm of illusion. As an adult, Hitchcock displaced his childhood terror by holding the public hostage to his anxiety, and thus
it is the public that is traumatized/fascinated by *Psycho*
and *The Birds*. In the latter film, a cloud of birds swoops
down on innocent people; horror is interwoven with fear
stemming from the past, and the terror is in the tone.

Ingmar Bergman is another past master of the horror film. In his childhood, too, there occurred an event

that, on the imaginary level, took on the value of a trauma
(see Terr 1987). Not quite five years old, he was playing at
his grandmother's house when he was accidentally locked
in a closet. While his grandmother was looking for the key,
the child ripped his mother's clothes with his teeth. The
traces of this early experience can be seen in his later fascination with imprisonment, corpses, and death. At the age
of six, he went with his father, a hospital guard, when the
father took dead people to the cemetery, and he was present
when amputated limbs were burned in blast furnaces, the
fascination with bodily disintegration joining the memory
of being shut up in the closet.

Bergman brought these experiences of near death
to the screen, transposing the original traumas. The
viewer is spared no horror, but his suffering is nevertheless accompanied by a yield of pleasure in the realm of
fantasy. Thus the early experience, caught up in the later
work of symbolization and mourning, is put into words
and thereby assumes the cultural role that Freud assigned
to children's play. In *Torment*, a film that combines panic
with malice, Bergman presents the story of a schoolmas-
ter who, having killed a young woman, hides behind some
clothing. In *Hour of the Wolf*, a child tells of being shut up
in a closet. In *A Ship Bound for India* and *Port of Call*, we
see boat cabins with the dimensions of prison cells, and
in later films Bergman imprisons characters in train com-
partments or traps them in an elevator. The knight in *The
Seventh Seal* is shut up in a medieval confessional together
with Death. The place in which a sinner is supposed to

be freed of his sins becomes a chamber of horrors, the closet in which Bergman had been locked as a child.

Similarly, Bergman's quasi-autobiographical film *Fanny and Alexander* shows children imprisoned by their stepfather in a small upstairs room; a friend rescues them by concealing them in a trunk. Discussing this scene, Terr mentions the psychological traumas experienced by children taken hostage in a kidnapping (I'll return to this later on). These captive children "visualize" the way in which they will be freed, and it is this process of visualization, with all its improbability, that is at work in this film. In other films, Bergman tried to recover the yield of pleasure associated with his trauma at age six when he accompanied his father from the hospital to the mortuary: in *The Magician* there is a severed hand; in *Shame* a disemboweled body lying on the ground; in *The Passion of Anna* a horse is burned and a dog tortured. As Terr observes, the tonality of Bergman's style is that of psychic trauma: terror, horror, panic, the feeling of absolute helplessness. The anxiety effects are contagious, and, prey to claustrophobia, we are ready to cry out.

Traumatized artists fascinate us. Freud (1915) poses the questions that Octave Mannoni (1968) sums up in these terms: How can the representation of suffering become a source of pleasure? Why do we feel compelled to repeat unpleasant situations, as in post-traumatic neurosis or children's play? Winnicott (1971) continues this investigation by examining the creative impulse itself, in which the work of art is located between the observer and the artist's creativity. But he concludes that the creative impulse itself can probably never be accounted for. What interests him, on the other hand, is the connection between creative life and life itself, and the reasons why this creative life may be lost.

In his study of war neuroses, Freud (1920) examines the effects on vulnerable people of external aggression and mortal danger, and discusses the enigma of repetition as exemplified by the *fort/da* game, in which the child repeats an unpleasant situation in order to master it. Freud shows how the dramatization of the episode brings about a link between the life instinct and the death instinct: the game makes possible the psychic elaboration of object loss. Eventually, in *Inhibitions, Symptoms, and Anxiety* (1926), Freud clearly distinguishes between the traumatic situation and the danger situation. In the former, anxiety is connected with the fear of being rendered helpless; in such a case, the feared danger may evoke prior traumatic experiences. The traumatic situation is essentially that of overwhelming abandonment anxiety.

### The Victims of the Chowchilla Kidnapping

Lenore Terr's (1979) study of the kidnapping of twenty-six California children in 1976 reveals the different responses of children and their families to one and the same traumatic event. Though the artist, thanks to his gifts, is able to create a new reality from a disturbing event, the layperson wants only to forget; it is in dreams that we find the repetition of the trauma that the waking subject tries to erase or banish from memory.

At the time of the kidnapping, the population of Chowchilla, a small rural community of 5,000 inhabitants, wanted to forget about it. Then, gradually, because they had to deal with nightmares and with the children's fears, the parents began to complain that they were not being helped. Lenore Terr met with four families in December 1976 and, until August 1977, undertook a study of twenty-three of the victims who had remained in Chowchilla with their parents. She set herself two goals: to offer brief treatment to the victims (while assessing which of them might require long-term therapy) and to learn as much as possible about the effects on the children and their families of a unique traumatic event.

The group of children comprised seventeen girls and six boys, ranging in age from five to fourteen. Fourteen of the families were very disadvantaged socioeconomically. Only one of the children was considered by his parents to have had behavioral problems before the event, but, in the course of her investigation, Terr realized that several other children had also suffered from more or less serious psychological disorders. One of the little girls had been suddenly separated from her father and lived in a state of depression, haunted by the fear of losing her mother as well; another, at the age of seven, had discovered the body of her young brother, who had been accidentally electrocuted, and was therefore, even before the kidnapping, suffering from post-traumatic anxiety; a third child was blind; another had severe asthma. And seven children were developmentally delayed to some extent.

On July 15, 1976, three masked men kidnapped twenty-six children on a bus bound for their summer school and held them hostage for twenty-seven hours, at the end of which time the children and the driver managed to escape. Terr describes how the children were transferred from the bus into two vans after most of the siblings had been separated from one another. The windows of the vans were painted over, and thus it was in darkness that the children were transported for eleven hours with no food, drink, or sanitary facilities; they were then placed in a hole. A masked man asked each child's name and took away personal items (T-shirts, eyeglasses, toys). Then they were taken to a larger, well lit area and given water and something to eat. Separate toilets for boys and girls were improvised.

The children remained in the hole for sixteen hours, during which time there was a moment of panic when a little boy of ten dislodged a post that was holding up the ceiling, which threatened to cave in. For several hours the driver, with the aid of some of the children, worked to dig out an exit, which required the lifting of a heavy metal sheet. Finally, at dusk, the driver helped the children to escape and managed to call the police from a phone booth and have the location of the call traced. The entire group was then taken to a nearby prison to undergo questioning and get some sleep. The next morning, the children were reunited with family members and had to face officials, reporters, and television cameras. They spent a total of thirty-six hours away from home, after which they had to be examined, prolonging the period of separation to forty-three hours.

## The Children's Reactions

Terr points out that, of the twenty-three children, only eight had been aware of danger. Several of the children had not known that they were being kidnapped. Others, overcome by anxiety, thought they saw a fourth kidnapper, though none existed, and the belief in a fourth criminal terrified them for some time. The transfer from the bus to the vans and then to the hole caused severe anxiety, especially in the children over the age of eight; some of them thought they were going to be shot. The eleven hours of traveling in the vans without being able to urinate caused urinary blockage lasting twenty-seven hours in some of the children and, in some cases, impairment of kidney function. During the time spent in the hole, some of the children fainted or felt they were suffocating; others experienced hallucinatory phenomena and the fear that they would never see their families again.

Some were reluctant to raise their heads out of the hole lest it be cut off. Even after the escape, the children continued to feel afraid. On the other hand, they did not experience the time in prison as traumatic, appreciating the opportunity to wash and to have clean underwear. The events preceding the kidnapping took on great retrospective importance, especially for those who had left their families after a fight. On the whole, we may conclude that denial was not at work: the children had understood that a drama was unfolding.

### The Long-Term Effects

Terr ascertained that twenty children feared that they would be kidnapped again, twelve were afraid of an alleged fourth kidnapper, and six feared that the arrested kidnappers would strike again after completing their sentences. Ten of the children could not bear to be left alone at home, fifteen were afraid of noise, three of confined spaces, and three of very large spaces, while eight were seized with uncontrollable anxiety in the course of which they would cry, call for help, or run away. Terr emphasizes that, for most of the children, trust in adults was irreparably shaken; some of them even showed fear of their parents, refusing to be kissed or to sit on the parents' laps. We may say that the kidnapping not only revived but also magnified archaic abandonment anxieties as well as fear of darkness and noise.

## *Psychodramatic Play*

Terr offered a "play space" for psychodramatic exploration of the kidnapping. Although some of the children
were able to enact their drama by identifying with the
aggressor, they were not freed from anxiety in so doing.
On the contrary, what characterized the game for over
half of them was its repetitiveness: unable to transcend
or transpose the terror, the child would often remain
imprisoned. The compulsive nature of the game, whether
on a stage or in televised interviews, involved the children's insistence that they not be interrupted. The story
was reeled off in a staccato monotone; when the adult
made a pause, the child would resume exactly at the point
where he or she had been interrupted.

Terr notes that the more extensively the traumatic
drama was staged, the more necessary it was that it be
interrupted from without, in the hope that at some time
the child would be able to free up the words walled in by
anxiety.

Some of the children were acting out, a year and a
half or two years later, in a way that related to the trauma:
for one of them, an attempted murder with a toy gun out
of fear of being kidnapped, for others a fire or acts of
revenge. The "heroes" of Chowchilla—the boys who had
actively helped the driver to arrange the escape—suffered
from severe post-traumatic distress, which is not the case
in similar situations where the victim was "active" or "heroic" (Horowitz 1976, cited by Terr). The post-traumatic

sequelae for the "heroes" of Chowchilla were the same as for the passive victims. In their play, both sets of children acted out the same horror of abandonment; as Terr points out, the "heroes" had first of all been victims.

### Dreams and Fantasies

The children's dreams collected by Terr were of four types: repetitive nightmares, sometimes followed by sleepwalking; nightmares that awoke the parents but the content of which was forgotten; repetitive dreams involving various episodes in the kidnapping and evoking in some of the children the feeling of being paralyzed or killed; and premonitory dreams, occurring nineteen months after the event, anticipating a repetition of the kidnapping.

The dreams of repetition reflect traumatic neurosis, except for the fact that the compulsion to repeat brought no relief. Terr tried to get the children to put their feelings into words, in the hope of rescuing the drama from oblivion so as to make a place for further psychic elaboration. But those children who had not mastered language remained unable to remember the content of their nightmares and were left with the paralyzing effects of their terror.

Some of the children developed revenge fantasies, while others took refuge in heroic and religious reveries and saw no value in speaking with Terr. The religious children cherished the memory of having been totally devoted to their companions. Still others projected their own hostility onto their parents, conjecturing that their mothers would have preferred them to remain in the hole.

## Physical Symptoms

Symptoms such as enuresis, cramps, asthma, nystagmus, and fainting were associated with difficulties the children had experienced prior to the kidnapping. The drama of the abduction, in the real, exacerbated symptoms or revived those that had disappeared.

Not only had each child undergone psychic trauma, but the family members were affected as well, via identification. Some of the parents developed fear of strangers, fear of a repetition of the traumatic event, or displacement of their hostility toward the kidnappers onto the school, the government, or other parents. The therapeutic assistance provided by Terr permitted abreaction of a terror that, once spoken about, became less intense in the nightmares. Six out of the twenty-six families moved from Chowchilla within a year, without leaving a forwarding address. As for the guilt of the children or the parents who had quarreled before the drama took place, it was extreme, each seeking after the fact to explain the event in terms of subjective factors such as a "premonition" or "signal" that a catastrophe was bound to occur.

Psychoanalytic understanding of the aggression that had befallen children and parents alike was aimed at re-establishing a psychic and physical container within which each victim could, through play and fantasy, transform and even overcome the distress of the event. The dramatization of the crisis allowed the real drama to become something else. A compromise between the events of the past and their current problematics came about by means of a transmission that made it impossible to repress the material.

The environment provides a child with continuity of being; hence aggression from without, in this case the kidnapping, introduced a break in the relation to the other and deprived the children of the support they needed in order to exist. The degree of distress, highly variable from one victim to the next, was closely tied to the feeling of safety that each had, or lacked, before the aggression. Somatization allowed hatred to diminish; on the level of fantasy, the subject, in the manner of primitive people, fears that death (or the enemy) is plotting revenge against him, and when depression abates, when its somatic coordinates disappear, persecutory elements likewise fade away. Only the mastery of anxiety enables a reinvestment of object libido. If the ego cannot accomplish this, the way out can only be suicide or mania, or the regressive solution of an anti-life.

Speaking of pain brings relief. There are extreme situations, such as internment in a concentration camp, in which even thirty years later the victims are still unable to speak of what happened to them as children. What remains unspoken is a wound that is handed down from generation to generation, a wound of memory the effect of which is to rob the victim of pleasure in life.

pushed away
covered
un mourned

# 2

## *The Survivors of Genocide*

The survivors of the roundups and internments perpetrated by the Nazis have a different understanding of their own childhoods and those of their children (Auerhahn and Laub 1987). Those who lived through the drama try to shift experience away from themselves (Bettelheim 1984), repressing memory until it returns and, literally, possesses them. They have not been able to mourn loved ones who were lost, or to feel grief. One cannot do so, Bettelheim points out, when one's own life is at risk, since this would get in the way of one's own survival. The only psychological possibility is denial, and some people do not allow themselves to feel the loss of a family member until thirty or forty years later, when they happen to meet a Holocaust crusader or an analyst and have the opportunity to speak to themselves in the presence of someone.

It is this refinding of memory that enables their children to lead a normal life.

One of the effects of the trauma of genocide is the victim's difficulty in establishing communication; he has lost the hope of being understood. It can therefore be hard to conduct analytic treatment with such patients. Some of them compulsively re-experience, in their analysis, the panic they had felt as children, the early fear of being shot having become, in the adult, a fear of death or persecutory anxiety. Memories themselves remain out of reach, and dreams are nonexistent. Often, as Auerhahn and Laub note, it is only in a second course of therapy, after these patients have been relieved and "loosened up" by their first analysts, that dreams and memories begin to arise. The survivors then want their own children to have a play space, so that the victims can reconnect with play through their children, an interaction between the self and the internalized other similar to the early mother–child relation. Analytic work brings about the restoration of a possibility of exchange between the self and others.

Auerhahn and Laub describe the case of a patient, Mr. B., whose parents were deported to the camps when he was four. A Catholic woman took him in and passed him off as her grandson. He had to conform to religious rituals but was allowed to pray before a photograph of his mother instead of before a crucifix. This photograph later took on the role of a transitional object for him, accompanying him on his travels and protecting him against an outer world that he experienced as hostile. Mr. B. thus clung to an idealized image of the parents he knew before their deportation. But his real parents had placed him in danger and aggravated his sense of persecution, and he had it in for them. When, as a child, Mr. B. found them after their return from the concentration camp, he could not connect those parents—emaciated, disfigured by torture, in prisoners' garb—with the parents whose idealized image he had kept within himself. Unable to accept these people as his parents, he spoke to them formally and impersonally.

Mr. B. had been able to cope during the war because his idealized image of his parents kept him safe; it was only upon their return that he acknowledged that they had really been deported. Once family security was reestablished, he allowed himself to be a child once again, that is, to break down: he had fever, insomnia, and repeated nightmares.

Later on, when he himself had a son, he bought the newborn infant an electric train and showered him with gifts. When his wife protested that the baby did not need all this, Mr. B. realized that he had bought these toys for himself and recalled the war years, when he had had none. For the adult Mr. B., the toys had taken on the value of transitional objects like the photo he had cherished as a child.

Some Holocaust survivors need their children to mother them. Others spend their free time so preoccupied with complicated toys (a sophisticated system of electric trains, for example) that they become enslaved by the rules for using them. This is not playful and creative relaxation but an obligation to do a job well, reproducing the forced labor in the camps under official gaze. In promoting play for their own children, these parents are trying to restore, even to repair, their own lost childhood. Yet they send their offspring a paradoxical message by forbidding them their right to make mistakes. In the game of life, they seem to say (cf. Auerhahn and Laub, p. 56), any mistake could prove fatal. With their opportunity for free invention constrained in this way and their world presented to them as basically threatening, the children likewise seek the protection of rules, as opposed to the laughter and improvisation of truly creative play.

By restricting themselves to "serious" educational pursuits and the necessity of "duty," such parents are unable to see that it is desire that motivates their children's play. Creativity is the condition for the subject's truth. In the absence of the field of play (O. Mannoni 1969) necessary for his unfolding, the subject may turn into the prototype of the model student, a slave to duty. Winnicott (1960) would say that the child is constructing a false self based on that of a mother who cannot locate herself on the side of life and fantasy, given her preoccupation with her own problems of hatred and death.

Through psychoanalysis, an adult can hope to escape the superego demand that prevents him from living. In the transferential space, we often see the patient projecting a deadly relation to the law; in an extreme case of such situations, the analyst is somehow controlled by a patient who is vigilantly making sure that the rules are correctly applied, from the absolutely fixed duration of sessions to the content of an interpretation. It often takes quite a while to "win over" the patient and give him permission to overcome his terror of the analytic play space, the space of free associations, dreams, and fantasies. It is by no means rare for the first phase of the treatment to take place *in front of* the analyst, who is excluded from the transferential field. This is a form of denial that immerses the patient in the drama of his own history.

As Freud pointed out, when we think we are innocent we are really guilty (cf. O. Mannoni 1968, p. 169), and guilt takes an even greater toll in the survivors of concentration camps. For if the normal person is a criminal in his infantile fantasies and death wishes, and if a prosecutor—in the person of the superego, agent of the death drive—has been installed in him, the survivor has even more difficulty in not feeling responsible for all the deaths in the camp. It is as though he owed his life to those deaths. Survivor guilt is often coupled with hatred for a parent who did not attempt to flee deportation, this hatred and the death drive then turning against the subject's own ego, accusing and torturing him. We often see more or less serious somatizations arising at the time when the survivor achieves a career, starts a family, or buys the house of his dreams. Somatization (depression, fractures, angina) can occur when the survivor reaches the age when his own parents were deported. "What did I do," the patient seems to be saying, "to deserve a better fate than my parents?" (cf. Eckstaedt 1984). It is only later, once this process of self-destruction has been undermined, that the patient is able to speak of the trauma experienced by his parents in the real and to bring to the surface the horror of long years of silence. To speak of these things is painful, for there remains the fear that the long-banished images of terror will overwhelm daily life and turn it into a nightmare.

The testimony of concentration camp survivors who are parents shows all the deadly effects of silence and secrecy into the second, even the third, generation. What is unspoken of the parents' terror weighs on their children, even when these children grew up in security in New York or elsewhere (cf. Epstein 1979). For each parent, the impossibility of speaking out is accompanied by unbearable guilt, as we see in the suffering of their children, whose neurosis bears witness to the parents' severance from the past. The younger generation is profoundly affected by the forbidding of knowledge concerning a page of history full of humiliation and horror.

The Nazi genocide had its repercussions in Argentina. There, in 1976, the military government arrested thirty thousand people, robbing them of their possessions, removing their children, and declaring them "disappeared." The children were adopted by childless military personnel, and all traces of the natural filiation were obliterated: the murderer of the father became the father of the orphan. For this coverup to succeed, for the father to be not so much "disappeared" as non-existent, the tacit agreement of the survivors was necessary. They were required to sign an official declaration of the "disappearance." To accept the disappearance, as Reinoso (1987) observes, was to *make it disappear, as if nothing had happened.*

It was to avoid complicity in the murders and child-snatching that, in 1977, a group of women defied the dictatorship and broke through the wall of silence by going to the governmental palace and claiming their children and grandchildren. By their presence, these mothers repealed the disappearance of the "disappeared," and their private resistance gradually became a public movement, one that made it necessary to inscribe something of life and death in the symbolic. The women wanted to know the names of the murderers and thereby denounce not so much the disappearance as the substitution of the murderer for the father.

The overturning of the military regime made it possible to search for the children stolen from their parents by the torturers. Some were returned to their family of origin; others were obliged to follow the procedure used in cases of divorce: returned to their family of origin, they nevertheless had regular visits with their adoptive family, the family of their parents' torturers. For these children, and the children they themselves would have, Reinoso asks, should we not fear a resurgence of murder in the real, if the relation to the truth is concealed in the symbolic?

Freud (1915) denounced the effect of this death that is killed by silence, the result of all wars, for it impoverishes life. In becoming the silent accomplice of a certain "order"—in this case, the arbitrariness of the Argentine military regime—a nation risks denying its children access to life, to the space of freedom necessary for invention and creation. The submission of the individual to the law is meaningful only if the law has not become a torture machine, that is, if society is founded on a basis other than terror and exclusion. As soon as the law becomes the embodiment of a killing machine, we are in a world where man excludes man, in a space where all difference is abolished. The "crazy women of the Plaza de Mayo"[1] demanded that the status of the dead be acknowledged. To say simply that these people had disappeared made it impossible for their families to mourn them, condemning the families to live in the past in the hope that their loved ones might return. In order for them to live in the present, there had to be a revelation not only of the thirty thousand murders (of which sixty-five percent of the victims were workers), but also of the abduction of children and the attack on their filiation through the substitution of the father's murderer for the father himself.

---

[1] In 1977 the Argentine women began to demonstrate silently every Thursday by walking around the pyramid in the Plaza de Mayo, a symbol of independence. Each one carried a handkerchief inscribed with the name and date of a disappearance. On the symbolic level, they were publicly supporting the *inscription* of the living or dead person.

"'The world has to know,' Rafael told us, 'that this deportation [during the Nazi occupation in the 1940s] marked us down to the third generation. . . . I didn't have a childhood; I don't have a mother any more; I have a sister who needs medical treatment and a father who was never able to live normally after he returned'" (Vegh 1984, pp. 118, 179). The accounts collected by Claudine Vegh have in common the fact that the children of survivors are immured in secrecy, sometimes for over thirty years. Several of them were able to admit the death of family members only after reading official records of the deaths. Similarly, it was only after the fact that one of the survivors, Sonia (pp. 119–128), became aware that she had gotten a divorce and become depressed at the age of thirty-four, the age at which her mother had been taken away. Her idealization of parents "who went away on a trip" was accompanied by a strong feeling of guilt, her superego becoming the agent of the death drive in the person of an accuser armed with instruments of torture. "I find it really hard to live beyond the time my mother lived," she said. The same was true for her brother, who passed his examinations but got himself expelled from the state educational system and worked occasionally as a painter and tiler, living on the margins of a society he rejected.

Another child of Holocaust victims, Jean (pp. 136–137, 181), tried to "start over again from square one" by erasing a past marked by the disappearance of his parents, his separation from his sister, and a childhood spent as a rejected orphan. After his marriage, he continued to have nightmares and to dream of his parents' return. There was no tomb at which he could contemplate their memory, only a single document: "Disappeared, Auschwitz 1943." "Oddly enough," he said, "I feel that I have no right to live." A past cannot be erased; its ghosts quickly catch up with you and break out into the real. Survival is experienced as a mistake, and the more heavily silence weighs on the trauma, the more the subject pays the price in various symptoms. It is only when the trauma is finally expressed in words that mourning can take place, and, as a result, reparative forces can be employed in the service of pleasure or simply of permission to live. Otherwise any success or satisfaction will produce depression, somatization, or the need for failure.

In the accounts she collected, Vegh notes the impact of the multiple separations and name changes some of the children had to undergo; this clandestine life, along with the uncertainty arising from the disappearance of the parents, caused severe trauma. "How will they find me again?" was a question often asked. And when, during vacations, some of the children who had had this same experience came together, they did not speak with one another. This rule, which was not imposed from without, stemmed from the repression and denial of grief and trauma.

At an age when identificatory processes were underway, the children discovered that their parents did not always attempt to resist or to escape: "They went like lambs to the slaughter," said Robert (p. 168), who held a grudge against them for this. And when the war was over and some children were reunited with parents who were humiliated, shabbily dressed, desperate, and terrified, they themselves became distraught, helpless, and appalled. As Vegh emphasizes, adolescent development is more difficult if the parents are unable to convey the sense of a history that takes shape in a cultural context. The child cannot accept himself as a Jew if being Jewish implies constant danger of death. Likewise, it is difficult to mourn dead parents when one feels that one is under threat of death oneself; if one is to stay alive the dominant feeling is one of refusal: "I resent the dead people who paid for my life with theirs. I can't live that way! They did nothing to stay alive," Robert declares; he feels like a criminal because, "after all, they're dead and I'm alive" (p. 168). Many years later, a dream would apparently put an end to this nightmare. This dream involved the farm in which his parents were buried, and the farm reminded him of a time when they had lived happily together, before the roundup. Those who finally had to admit that their vanished relatives were dead were deprived of the rituals that every social group has created in order to assist survivors. As Bettelheim (1984) notes, it isn't the dead but the living who need respect to be paid to the corpses.

The analyst treating a survivor of genocide knows that, before exploring other paths, he has to listen carefully to the horror experienced in reality. It is this horror that will refashion, transform, what was most conflictual in the patient's past. One patient killed himself when the analyst was away on vacation. Upon his return from captivity, he had realized that life on the farm where he had lived before had gone on without him; he had not only lost his place as the elder son but was convinced that he had been robbed of his possessions. No one had expected him to be alive, and he was now in the way. The separation from the analyst heightened his feeling of abandonment, a feeling that was also associated with ongoing jealousy of his younger brother. He had, in fact, lost the will to live well before his entry into analysis and hovered between life and death once he no longer had a container for his hatred. He rejected the idea of hospitalization, not without first raising to crisis level his feeling of worthlessness.

The transferential relationship requires an analyst who can win over the patient, as Winnicott would say, as opposed to wrapping himself in a silence that is too close to the experience of terror. An appeal is made, and a response is called for. In the case in question, this appeal for help was heard by the analyst, but the analyst failed in not getting the patient to agree to short-term hospitalization. For this patient, the very idea of hospitalization (or merely of placement with a rural family) was tantamount to a rejection: people were trying to get rid of him, to send him to a branch of Auschwitz. If the analyst had been able to accept the transferential role of executioner, he might have been able to prevent the patient from turning his murderousness against himself.

Analytic procedure must manage to free itself from rigid conventions that, for such patients, can recall those of the camps, so that these survivors can refind the play space of childhood. Only then can there be access to the patient's inner world as it overcomes terror and opens out onto the possibility of restoring the image of the self.

# 3

## *The Scene of Fantasy*

Once Freud became interested in fantasy, he set about describing the fantasmatic scenarios that the subject constructs for himself. Among these is the "family romance" (Freud 1909; cf. Laplanche and Pontalis 1973, 1985): children like to invent a more glamorous set of parents in order to be able to idealize those they sometimes find themselves angry at, or to get rid of them and take on the role of a new and more nobly born person. In his clinical practice, Freud constantly sought the original elements of the imaginary scenario in which the subject tries to grasp the enigma of his history through representations that, as in myths, provide an answer to his question.

Unconscious fantasies, Freud (1908b) explains, were once daydreams that, now forgotten, have fallen into the unconscious under the effect of repression. Freud compares the daydream to a serial novel in which the subject tells his story and is represented by its images. We may recall that Freud (1908a) compares children's play to the activity of the writer: like the writer, the child at play creates a personal world according to a new order. Freud describes the imaginary creations of adults—like reveries—as extensions or transpositions of the child's play. "In this domain reserved to fantasy, there is room for masterpieces as well as mistakes" (O. Mannoni 1968, p. 117). But, as Freud himself observes, the analyst does not know what it is that makes such works succeed or fail.

Although this is hardly their concern, artists open out a path toward knowledge of the unconscious. Shakespeare, as Octave Mannoni (1968) observes, helped Freud to discover the Oedipus complex but did not need, himself, to know more about it in order to speak of it. Right from the start, Shakespeare was able to inscribe himself, from a point of opacity, as a participant in a drama, for creativity requires some degree of dramatization. Why are some people content with just their daydreams, while others are driven by the desire to write in order to feel alive? This desire often stems from an intense experience that must be worked through again if a traumatic situation is to be resolved (M'Uzan 1977, pp. 3–27). The opacity of some narratives reveals that even if the author did not understand what was happening to him, his unconscious knew. The complexity of a situation or the evocation of a conflict can be admirably presented in this way.

Daniel Paul Schreber, president of an appellate court, published his *Memoirs* in 1903, after a long psychiatric hospitalization. With genuine literary talent, he describes a fantastic universe in which, believing he was called upon to become a woman, he was present at the birth of a new human race. This delusional reconstruction of the world was an attempt at self-cure on his part. Schreber clearly explains how his hallucinations contain an objective truth that only he can perceive, and he agrees to be considered mentally ill, to claim his right to his delusion, in the conviction that when the world is destroyed he, as a woman, will play an integral part in a new humanity.

The autobiographical link to his own life points to one truth, psychoanalysis to another. Schreber examines his own fate, his grand struggle and his defeat, finally accepting himself in a world ruled by what he calls his hallucinations. His book, ostensibly an indictment of arbitrary institutionalization, is at the same time a plea for the right to madness. He unquestionably succeeds in going beyond his own imprisonment in delusion to give the reader a literary document of rare quality. Writing confirmed his right to existence, as the real father is replaced by the power of a new universe that grants a place to the son as a woman. The creative process here involves a dramatic production that makes us, as readers, aware of how at a certain stage of life we, like Schreber, could feel crushed by the educational, familial, and judiciary systems. The construction of a new reality, a delusional

world in which he could live, enabled Schreber to overcome the traumatic experience.

A student of languages, in his rage to destroy his
mother tongue, has given us another wonderful book
(Wolfson 1970), one in which, as Gilles Deleuze notes in
his Preface, we can see a special sort of health beginning
to take form in the depths of the illness. The author cannot bear to hear his mother speak and therefore begins
to convert the words of his native language into foreign
ones. At the end of the book, he manages to get enough
distance from his anxiety about death and destruction to
be able to say, "And there is even some hope that, in the
end, . . . one day the young man who is mentally ill will
once again be able to use that language, the famous English language, in a normal way" (p. 247). Nevertheless,
his reconciliation with his parents takes place through the
use of Yiddish with his mother, French with his father.
Thus protected from his destructive impulses by taking
shelter in a language other than the maternal one, he can
approach his family without fear of committing a crime.

Literary history, as Michel de M'Uzan (1977, p. 10)
reminds us, can turn to its own account Freud's observa-
tion that there is no true achievement without a bit of
criminality. If the usual run of humanity contents itself
with daydreaming, the artist—psychotic or not—draws
from his inner life the material for fantasy representations
with which he can comfort others and give pleasure to
them (cf. Freud 1916–1917, p. 376). Poets and novelists,
Freud (1907) tells us, know many things of which we, with

our formal education, are ignorant, and they are further along than we are in their knowledge of psychology.

Thus the novelist can enable us to understand some basic principles of psychopathology. Pirandello, for example, in his 1904 novella *The Late Mattia Pascal*, describes the experience of rebirth of a young librarian. Overwhelmed by an unhappy marriage and an unsatisfactory way of life, Mattia leaves his sad provincial town, tries his luck at Monte Carlo, and wins a small fortune. On the way back, he reads in a newspaper that a corpse had been found in his town and identified as his. Declared officially dead, he at first thinks of correcting the misunderstanding but then considers that he now has a lot of money that he can keep for himself and, as a "dead" man, no debts, no wife, no mother-in-law. He is free! The miraculous chance that allowed him to escape legal existence leads him, once he has savored the joy of reading the obituary and feeling himself to have been loved and missed, to take on a new identity. He sheds his past and gives birth to a new man with a new family history.

Wiping out the traces of Mattia Pascal in himself, he changes his appearance with the help of a barber. He is stuck with certain facial features that displease him, but elegant eyeglasses, a new long hairdo, a frock coat, and a wide-brimmed hat give him the look of a German philosopher. Then, in the train taking him far from his native town, Mattia overhears a name mentioned in a conversation and, as in a baptism, takes it as his own: Adriano Meis. With childlike joy he begins a new life. But he needs parents, grandparents, the sense of a lineage. In spite of himself, the origins he invents for himself have their roots in the soil in which he grew up. Mattia Pascal had lost his father at the age of four and a half and had remained alone with an older brother along with a mother who was anxious, intrusive, and incapable of managing the fortune her husband had left her. Mattia experienced his father's death as an abandonment that led to the family's ruin. What father, then, could he give to Adriano Meis, an only son?

Adriano wants to be as unique as possible. But he has to find a birthplace: on a steamship, for example, or in South America. Yes, he was born in America, the son of a bad type who abandoned his wife as she was about to give birth. Orphaned at an early age, he had been brought back to Italy to be raised by his grandfather. He cannot profane his mother's memory by inventing another mother for himself—but a grandfather, yes, a cultured old gentleman who introduced him to the arts. After visiting Milan, Padua, Venice, Florence, and Perugia, Adriano settles in Rome. His landlord, a man of about sixty, accompanies him on countless walks through the city, speaking of death; his meditations cut him off from all material existence.

Once the exhilaration of freedom has passed, Adriano becomes aware of the gap between fantasy and reality. In turning into his own ideal—a process Freud (1914) describes as a substitute for the lost narcissism of childhood—he has cut himself off from the world and from any possibility of love. To protect his usurped identity, he has managed only to live a lie. But saying "I am lying" affirms his will to deceive (cf. Lacan 1964) and implies a truth that endangers him. He soon finds himself isolated psychologically in such a way that his relations with reality cause him distress. His wandering eventually leads to his becoming solitary and silent: Where is he, as a subject, in what he shows to the world? Caught in this doubling of himself, in the net of illusion, Adriano becomes disoriented in his disguise and develops a bitterness toward others that works as a poison on himself (cf. Lacan 1964).

Adriano discovers that the freedom into which he had plunged has its limits and involves a deception. His feeling of omnipotence gives way to depression. He now accuses his wife and his mother-in-law of having forced him to accomplish what they had decided to do: they have succeeded in killing him, in getting rid of him. After two years of drifting, he has no choice but to kill his puppet Adriano Meis, to drown him in turn. At the darkest spot along the Tiber, he throws his hat into the water, leaves a ticket and his cane on the parapet, and flees. Mattia Pascal can come back to life.

Having killed Adriano, the late Mattia tries to regain his relation to his own body image, to connect the passion that had linked him to the persona of Adriano to what he himself had been before being declared dead. Mattia had been dissatisfied with the imperfections of this body with its odd facial features. But never mind: Mattia, separated from his pathological role as Adriano, decides to reconcile with the part of himself that his relatives and friends had mourned at his graveside. No longer able to live like a hunted animal, under a usurped name and without civil status, he returns to his native town like a traveler who has been away for a long time without sending news of himself. He meets his brother, his own wife, who has remarried, and his mother-in-law.

But the joy of the reunion is clouded by the fact that his presence disturbs a social order that had re-established itself without him. In the eyes of his family, Mattia is like a ghost from the land of the dead, arousing anxiety: suddenly fantasy and reality merge, as the fantastic rises up and causes amazement. Why, Mattia cries out, are the people who mourned his death now weeping because he is alive? He begins to see that regaining his civil status as a living man will bring about the annulment of his wife's marriage to his rival, while he himself will have to deal with his hated mother-in-law. Mattia therefore resigns himself to ending his life as "the late Mattia Pascal." He finds refuge with an old aunt, and a priest finds him work as a librarian and keeps the secret of his rebirth under the seal of the confessional. "Your story shows that outside the law of the land, and apart from those little happenings, painful or pleasant as they may be, which make each of us what we are, my dear Pascal, life is impossible," the priest tells him (p. 320).

Mattia Pascal, having ended the life of his double, Adriano Meis, agrees to his own symbolic death as he ends his days in the shadow of the Mattia Pascal to whom his fellow townspeople had set up a gravestone. When asked who he is, he replies, "the late Mattia Pascal." It is impossible, Pirandello tells us, to do away with human limitation and contingency; we can neither erase our past nor escape our origins.

The fantasy of self-creation stems from early traumas (Rittenberg and Shaw 1991); in the Pirandello story, it was the early death of the father. Edgar Allan Poe lost his parents at the age of two and, in adolescence, fell into a deep depression after the death of a friend's mother. At the age of twenty-seven, he lost his fourteen-year-old wife to tuberculosis, the same disease that had taken his parents from him. He sank into delirium followed by alcoholism. And yet it was with this powerful destructiveness and passion that he gave the best of himself in his work. Pirandello, Poe, and E. T. A. Hoffmann (cf. Freud 1919), among others, arouse shock in the reader, who finds himself with the feeling of uncanniness that has its source outside of experience but brings forth elements that we take for reality. When we become aware of the deception, Freud (1919) notes, it is already too late; the author has achieved his aim. In ordinary life we tend to be passive with regard to our experience, but fiction produces different effects and brings a significant bonus of pleasure.

This excess of pleasure is found in the theater, the place of illusion in which performers act within conventions that must be respected if the theatrical effect is to be maintained (cf. O. Mannoni 1988, pp. 14–15): if the actor pretending to be dead does not move, this is so that the spectator will not notice that he is not really dead. Like the author, the actor onstage creates in the public the feeling that what they are experiencing is even more true than the play being presented. Octave Mannoni (1988, pp. 23–25) located the origin of the theater—but the same is true for the novel—in *boredom.* The viewer or reader is someone to whom nothing happens, someone who seeks to live vicariously through the hero. The hero is an ideal; the various characters in the play represent different aspects of the ego, keeping in reserve all the lives that we might have, and the very word *stage* has become the term for the psychic location in which images strut about.

The writer works with an internal force—the public or the father—with whom he maintains relations that will bear on the very process of creation (cf. M'Uzan 1977, pp. 20–21). He sometimes has the feeling that he is usurping a position and wielding, megalomaniacally, a power over the life and death of the characters he creates. The double quickly becomes the persecutory enemy of the hero, whose sleep he troubles to the point of driving him to madness (cf. Rank 1914, referring to Dostoyevsky's *The Double*). Elsewhere the double is like a reflection stolen from the mirror, or it is the very embodiment of the clinical picture of paranoia.

In 1914, Freud abandoned the notion of the ego as the agent of adaptation and made it an image, the vestige of past identifications, "the agent of madness at least as much as of reason" (O. Mannoni 1968, pp. 151–152). Artistic talent remained an enigma for Freud, but he did note that someone who is able to transform his fantasies into artistic creations instead of into symptoms thereby escapes neurosis and affirms his relation to reality. Freud is amazed at the insight of writers whose clinical descriptions often go beyond what the scientific knowledge of the times can provide.

In their article, "Fantasies of self-creation," Rittenberg and Shaw (1991) pay homage to the psychological perceptiveness of such writers and, as a counterpoint, give examples of self-creation from their own clinical work. The first case is that of a forty-two-year-old businessman, admired for his success in his line of work. Less fortunate in love, he had been married twice and had custody of the children by both wives. His social success was a façade, an over-adaptation concealing genuine distress, particularly with regard to his identity. He constantly wondered whether to change his careers, his women, his place of residence. He entered analysis with the question of how he could refashion himself.

His truth was obscured by a very complex relation of fantasy and desire. One scenario predominated, in which he was all-powerful and trusted no one besides his mother. The authors draw the exact parallel between this patient's childhood and that of Mattia Pascal: both, at the age of four and a half, had experienced a loss—the departure of their fathers for war. When the father returned, the child remained the exclusive object of a paranoid

mother who controlled his body intrusively and manically
until he was much older. In his desire to free himself from
the symbiotic ties to a mother experienced as persecutory, the patient, from early on, developed a fantasy in
which he became the origin of his own history. In this
scenario of desire, he was rid of his parents and identified with Superman, living in a kingdom that had its own
language and its own laws. Once the parents were out of
the way, he became his own creator. As an adolescent, he
envisioned himself as an adult surrounded by women who
were the sole survivors of a war and to whose sexual whims
he submitted. Later on, he extended the forced labor that
he imposed on himself in his professional life to his lei-
sure time, establishing a master–slave relationship with
an active fantasy of the death of the powerful woman.

This patient wanted analysis to rid him of his past
once and for all, so that he could become a completely
different person, an uncastratable man. He thereby forgot the illusory nature of a power that is conferred only
outwardly and failed to acknowledge that, as Lacan puts
it, the subject does not coincide with his own reality (1966,
pp. 94–95). In attempting to impose his own will on the
world and to triumph over what he perceived to be the
disorder around him, the patient managed, in Lacan's
words, "to enclose his existence in a circle, except if he
breaks through it by some violence in which, striking a
blow against what seems to him to be disorder, he hits
himself through the social repercussions" (1966, p. 172).

The other patient discussed by the authors was a forty-six-year-old writer who sought analysis because of emotional problems with his eight-year-old son. Was he, the patient, male or female, a writer or an impostor? Identified with a depressive mother, he took on the role of "housewife," his wife working outside the home. As a child, he had been symbiotically tied to his mother while his father was away on business trips. But at the age of four, as in the preceding case, the patient withdrew into a fantasy in which the theme was his self-creation: he became someone else, freed from his parents. Later, when he himself became a father, he began to feel like an impostor and a "fairy." In his fantasies he had a uterus, and, on the somatic level, he developed a bleeding ulcer. He even fantasized about giving birth and becoming his own mother. The obverse of these fantasies consisted of fantasies of destruction.

The authors emphasize that, in all these clinical examples of self-creation, there is an identification with the mother and, ultimately, a wish to be rid of both parents. What strikes me as important in these cases is the difficulty these men had in assuming the role of father. Lacan (1958), alluding to the beliefs of an Australian tribe, explains that although, in reality, people are aware that a woman cannot have a child without having had intercourse, "if the symbolic context requires it, paternity will nonetheless be attributed to the fact that the woman met a spirit at some fountain or some rock in which he is supposed to live" (p. 199). Thus Lacan goes on to say that "the attribution of procreation to the father can only be the effect of a pure signifier," and he recalls that Freud connected

> the appearance of the signifier of the Father, as author of the Law, with death, indeed with the murder of the father, thus showing that, if this murder is the fertile moment of death through which the subject binds himself for life to the Law, the symbolic Father is, insofar as he signifies this Law, the dead Father. [p. 199, translation modified]

When the father fails to come into being on the symbolic level, what remains? There remains, as Lacan tells us, the imaginary relation, which is not inscribed in a triangular dialectic. If the relation to the real person is reduced to an image, what is left is a function of specular alienation "that will exist in the inordinate relation of a person appearing merely in the order of power and not in the order of a pact."[1] Lacan sees a dehumanizing element in this imaginary relation. The subject will bear the brunt of the annihilation of the paternal signifier throughout his life, "through a series of purely conformist identifications with people who will give him the feeling for what one has to do to be a man." Thus "psychotics

1. Personal notes taken at Lacan's seminar of April 18, 1956; cf. Lacan 1955–1956.

can live compensated lives, . . . and then all of a sudden, mysteriously, God only knows why, they decompensate" (Lacan 1955–1956, p. 205, translation modified).

The patients discussed by Rittenberg and Shaw, like Pirandello's hero, are impostors: triumphantly occupying a position founded on the annihilation of one's parents does not help the subject to construct his own identity. On the contrary, the megalomania and omnipotence give way to depression, and this can lead to symbolic or real suicide. The difficulty for the writer who unconsciously bases his work on the elimination of the real father is, as Michel de M'Uzan says, "to come to terms with a megalomaniacal usurpation of power, the first effect of which is a destructive act" (1977, p. 21). Creativity is motivated by a present event combined with what of the past can be transposed, recreated, on an Other stage. This stage, which cannot be located in the psychic apparatus, "is just as welcoming, if not more so, to fantasy and reverie as it is to the hallucination of the dream" (O. Mannoni 1968, p. 117). What, Octave Mannoni (1969) asks, could be the meaning of a work that would make sense only in one life? He thus underlines the relations of the work not only to the author's life, but also to the lives of others, to our life, in its quest for what lies hidden.

# 4

## Creativity and Play in the Child

"Our linguistic intelligence," Octave Mannoni tells us, "is at its highest level at the age of two. It is at this age, and perhaps even before, when no one is able to explain anything methodically to us, that we begin to understand the meaning of the words that we hear" (1988, p. 76). Later on, this linguistic intelligence—the intelligence that enables young children to pick up foreign languages quickly, without having to learn grammar and syntax— begins to disappear, and thus the most talented linguists are those who have kept in contact with that early childhood achievement.

Octave Mannoni, noting the importance of rhythm (which we know well before the advent of speech), quotes Feyerabend on the way in which children play with words "until they discover a meaning that is beyond their reach" (1988, p. 84). It is in this activity that Feyerabend locates the early origins of inventiveness. He contrasts child's play with the performance of translating machines, legal language with poetry. The poet seeks to rediscover "the childhood experience of speech," while the linguist would prefer to rediscover "the almost intuitive understanding of the time when we were assimilating our parents' language" (O. Mannoni 1988, p. 86). From this point of view, Lewis Carroll would be closer to the language games of the poet. This kind of speech is what Freud (1900) locates in the dream, where it says nothing outright but yet indicates what it holds back from saying.

It is through play that Freud (1908a) approaches the question of daydreaming and shame. The adult, he tells us, is ashamed of his fantasies, feeling them to be childish and forbidden. And he wonders whether we may truly compare the creator of literature to the daydreamer. He notes that the author identifies with his hero and personifies his own conflicts through various protagonists while regarding the other characters from outside; he is thus both actor and spectator. Every literary work—and the same is true of the various forms of creativity in the child—belongs to a specific moment in the life of its author, yet the author tends to fade into the background as subject when he produces the work. He projects himself into characters that he brings to life and writes for someone who becomes the support for his relationship to himself. "No one," Octave Mannoni writes, "has a monopoly on meaning" (1988, p. 61); everyone has blind spots. Reading, and the communication of the author with the reader, take place against the background of resistances, of secrets to be disguised, and of a dimension of the unnamed that needs to be respected.

Ellen Handler Spitz (1987) movingly evokes the songs composed by George Crumb (1970) to the texts of five poems by Federico Garcia Lorca. These songs attempt to convey what is most archaic in the mother–infant relation, namely that difficult transition from dependence to independence, begun in the first year of life (cf. Winnicott 1945). The progress toward independence is constantly accompanied by turning back to a twofold dependence, since the mother sometimes finds it hard to let her baby grow up outside her. This passage can take place only if, at the beginning, the mother can identify with her baby enough to guess its needs, its sorrows, its discomforts. Later, when the child's intellectual awakening helps her to get back to a life of her own, the mother still harbors some nostalgia for the time when the infant fulfilled her and seemed to be an extension of her own being. It is this nostalgia that is evoked in Crumb's *Ancient Voices*. The original choreographic spectacle, using the most diverse instruments such as cymbals, tambourine, and Japanese temple bells, can be equally well adapted to pantomime. Silence and absence are juxtaposed, now in harmony, now in dissonance. The music and drama, Spitz tells us, bring us back to an archaic phase of our own life.

According to Spitz, the distant voices, sustained by the lamentation of oboes and magnified by pianos in reso-

nance with the drums of Tibetan prayers, evoke the inter-
weaving of the ancient and the primitive. The mixture of
human and instrumental sounds gives way to a voice that
rings out in all directions. From the void there arise the
words of a mother calling for her child, as though she were
trying to re-establish contact with the child in herself—not
only the child she brought into the world, but also her own
child-self. In counterpoint, another voice affirms a redis-
covered identity. The spectator is carried along by the conflicts and the troubles that can be heard in the play of jux-
tapositions in the musical score.

The separations of birth and death are marked by
maternal voices, alternating with heartrending laments
about the deaths of children. The composer and the
actors depict a primitive state of undifferentiation, the
organization of the world as it is structured for the individual by the narcissistic wounds, bereavements, and separations that underlie the constitution of his identity and
the resulting apprehension of reality.

This primitive undifferentiation (cf. Bleger 1981)
is like a structure, an organization including the subject
and his environment, that has its own dynamic with
pathological and "normal" moments in the development of the personality. Strongly influenced by Margaret Mahler (1963), Spitz experienced the beauty of this
musical performance, described in Mahlerian terms, as
the practical application of a theory. The performance,
in this view, deals with the birth process, in the course
of which the baby passes from a state of "unity" with the

mother to that of individuality, a process that Winnicott (1945) calls integration/disintegration. Integration— birth into a body differentiated from that of the mother— appears only gradually from an unintegrated state. In contrast to disintegration, Winnicott says, unintegration is not frightening.

The performance of which Ellen Handler Spitz writes seems to arouse in the spectator a kind of uneasiness along with a sense of strangeness. The imaginary anxieties, passions, and terrors depicted on this dream-stage then have a cathartic effect (O. Mannoni 1988, pp. 366– 371). The most original episodes, as Spitz describes them, involve the drama of birth and the process by which the mother identifies with the unborn child who is destined to separate from her in order to find his own identity, his own words. This baby must initially seek his own voice out of silence, independently of his mother's voice, creating a circle of inclusion and exclusion. Spitz relates that a soprano voice, representing the mother identified with a little boy, accompanies it in this quest. Then the baby is promised a ring so that he can wear his mother's silence on his finger without having to speak: the subject is given the time to find his own voice one day.

At one point the mother speaks in an aside to the audience:

I have lost myself in the sea many times,
with my ear full of freshly cut flowers,
with my tongue full of love and agony.

I have lost myself in the sea many times,
as I lose myself in the heart of certain children.
[quoted in Spitz 1987, p. 539]

These words, spoken (not sung) without musical accompaniment, are, the author suggests, a commentary on the thematic development that follows: we are already open to sound, to the voice; our ears and eyes are receptive, and we can lose ourselves in the music. The freshly cut flowers with which the voice fills our ears are the notes and words that have died once they pass the singer's lips.

Another episode involves the lament of a sterile woman who desperately hoped for a child. A musical dialogue is set up between two soprano voices, one being an adult woman who is onstage, the other a young man who is absent; the child remains invisible. The last part of the play is preceded by silence that, according to Spitz, represents death, the ultimate absence: every afternoon a child dies in Granada. The music evokes a loss that we must accept, a mourning we have to accomplish, at each phase of life—what Mahler (1963) calls a lifelong mourning process in which, at each stage, a certain quality of relationship has to be given up, never to be found again. The final words of the poem are sung, and by a child who comes onstage for the first time. The circle closes when the soprano walks toward him and they find, together, the wordless sounds of the beginning. This is a recapitulation of the opening moments of the play, the author tells us, communicated in a shared joy and serenity: the search within oneself for lost childhood.

Poetry, Octave Mannoni (1969) observes, does not lie in what one has to say. The richness of the performance described by Spitz lies in what it can evoke in each of us; it is ultimately irrelevant that it can be presented as an illustration of Mahlerian theory. George Crumb's setting to music of Garcia Lorca's poems awakens what is most deeply repressed in us, using silence and absence, which are sustained only by language, to create an opening into poetry.

Winnicott notes that "the patient's creativity can be only too easily stolen by a therapist who knows too much" (1971, p. 57). In the performance that Spitz describes, we come to understand through the poetry the voice of the child in search of himself and the drama of the mother who, as soon as her child is born, must mourn what she had carried inside her. The separation concerns both the baby and the mother, or mother-substitute. "Playing is doing," says Winnicott, "and *doing things takes time*" (1971, p. 41; italics in original). The play space or potential space, separating and uniting at the same time, varies from one baby to the other. The game is risky, with continuity assured by the frame provided by the mother or her substitute. The mother's inventiveness and her pleasure in sharing the baby's babbling, word play, and rhythmic songs call forth her child's creativity. Winnicott considers this creative experience to be "a basic form of living" (p. 86), and, in child analysis, "the significant moment is that at which *the child surprises himself or herself.* It is not the moment of my clever interpretation" (p. 51; italics in original). This holds true for pedagogy as well. We live at a time when increasingly sophisticated toys are thought up in order to increase the intelligence of tiny infants. Yet it is with a piece of string, and at unexpected times, that the child will truly discover the world if he is healthy, that is, in a state of inner security. It is also the case, however, that the string that promotes creativity for one child can be used by another child if he is anxious, as a way to deny separation through pathological exercises in mastery and control.

# — 5 —

# *The Life of the Imagination:*
# *Joys and Hazards*

In contrast to Melanie Klein, Winnicott attached great importance to the role of the environment in early life, since the quality of this environment, the exchanges between an infant and an adult who enjoys playing with it, have a major effect on later development. Those who are called schizophrenics, although they have lost contact with external reality, lead a life they consider happy. They can weave, paint, or take care of horses as long as they feel well (that is, safe) where they are living. On the other hand, so-called "normal" people can lose contact with their inner life. They are perfectly adapted and well behaved but incapable of creativity or of enjoying the zest and pleasures of life.

As Winnicott (1971) points out, extroverts who are unable to enter into contact with dreams are not fully happy. In a decathected psychic space there is no room for imagination. The mother-part no longer exists; it is experienced as dead and leaves what André Green (1986) calls a blankness in the psyche. In such cases, the subject cannot create. He seeks security by filling in a hole on the fantasmatic level, taking on obligations and restrictions that leave him no time to think. The fantasy activity of a patient of Winnicott's (1971) enabled her to dissociate to the point where she was no longer present in the world, while at the same time she was totally preoccupied by "doing," filling up her time with obligatory reading and painting as a defense against a continual threat of breakdown.

The importance Winnicott accords to the maternal environment is based on the need for feeling safe on the level of being, in a symbiotic relation with the other, before feeling safe enough to risk being alongside the other. For Winnicott, as for Lacan and Dolto, future identificatory possibilities are derived from the period before the separation from the mother's body. It is from the time of successful separation, when the child "has himself" in a body that belongs to him, that projective and introjective identifications can be established. Playing is doing, says Winnicott (1971), but André Green (1986) makes it clear that doing and playing are different, because playing presupposes the bringing into play of subjective creativity. For Winnicott, play is closer to dreaming—with its infinite possibilities for displacement—than to fantasy, which, for some, stems from a need to control the environment. He was most interested in the aspects of creativity that involve unformed experience, as in his use of "squiggles" that allow the child to enter a dream space and develop a life of the imagination (cf. O. Mannoni 1980).

Defending a kind of right to freedom, Winnicott mistrusted technical purity and believed that strict methods did not result in successful treatment. "The unconscious subject," Octave Mannoni adds, "has neither sex nor pretentions. Its activity is play, on the principle of the *Witz* (joking) and squiggles. Seriousness is the business of the ego, and thus, sometimes, of the false self" (1980, p. 132). Recalling the metamorphosis of Pierre Bezukhov in *War and Peace* (Tolstoy 1872, pp. 1285–1288), Octave Mannoni liked to speak of one of Tolstoy's final images, that of a man who, after many long trials, gains a wisdom of the heart that enables him to understand the language of the oppressed, of women, and of children. Pierre teaches his wife how to care for an infant, feeding it, doting on it, and playing with it, thereby putting an end to the succession of nurses they had had for their first baby, who was always sick. What he learned from his years of war, captivity, and suffering is that nothing matters more than regaining freedom in a situation in which one can create, change one's life, and love. At the end of the novel, he cares in a *motherly* way for a baby, an image of happiness that would no doubt have charmed Winnicott.

There are, then, two very different types of upbringing: one based on appearances and success at any price, and taking only reality into account; the other leaving the individual the time to seek himself, to find his path in a direction that guarantees the quality of human relations. In that space, there is room for gaiety and fantasy. It is at the end of a journey that had confronted him with so much hatred and crime that Pierre Bezukhov felt the need for another order, one that could create values radically different from those in which he had been brought up. His pleasure in the discovery of life's simple joys placed him, Lacan would say, on the side of the troubadours: "What is found is sought, but sought in the paths of the signifier. Now, this search is . . . beyond the pleasure principle" (1959–1960, pp. 118–119).

Freud, for his part, tried to account for certain activities supported by desire—activities, like artistic creation, involving the displacement or transformation of a sexual aim (Laplanche and Pontalis 1973, pp. 431–434). Thus he emphasizes the pleasure that is derived from successful sublimation (cf. Hartmann 1955). But for Winnicott it is the idea of pleasure in life—even a disordered life—that is of interest if the individual is to blossom forth. He raises Lacan's idea to another level: the infant *does not find the object* if the environment does not give him the opportunity to be alive amid the objects surrounding him. Creative play and self-fulfillment arise from moments of relaxation. It is this process, leading to self-realization, that is described in *War and Peace.* Pierre travels the difficult path from the false self to the true self, but not everyone can do so without the help . . . of an analyst!

Ernst Kris (1955) has attempted to explain the creative process by observing two- or three-year-old children as they paint. In the kindergarten that these children attended were an assortment of paints and large brushes. Kris describes controlled, disciplined children who proceeded methodically to mix colors in the paint pots before "attacking" the sheet of paper and gradually becoming bolder. For others, the daubing did not start for ten or twelve minutes. An "explosive" process set in with a certain arousal, the children tapping their feet, touching their genitals, and smearing the paint with fervor. Some, however, were so eager to "attack" the paper and make holes in it that the anxiety that underlies oral sadism, the fear of being flooded by excitation, prevented them from taking pleasure in painting.

The choice of colors was overdetermined. Thus one little boy, Tommy, chose brown despite his teacher's efforts to suggest another color. He had become aware of his mother's pregnancy and then, at the age of sixteen months, witnessed the death of the baby a few days after its birth. When Tommy was twenty-six months old, his mother, pregnant once again, had a miscarriage. The child then began to stutter and became increasingly anxious, and it was in this context that, full of rage, he found refuge in the color of excrement.

Desire seeks the release of tension. When this does not occur, the subject unconsciously invents ways to play with his desire and find release, and this cannot happen when the human environment does not respond appropriately. Emotion shared with others passes through language and thus allows for the symbolization of what was experienced, but not always understood, by the child. Yet how could one find the words to tell a sixteen-month-old child that the new baby is dead? And to tell him, later, of the loss of the baby that mother was carrying? The emotional climate of this family drama is that of a triangle: the child, the mother, and the father (or his substitute), and it is this structure that either does or does not provide security for the child by creating the symbolic matrix he needs to locate himself in the circuit of human exchanges with its moments of harmony, dissonance, enjoyment, and inventiveness.

In the case of Tommy, as described by Kris, we are able to see the transformation that painting can produce in a child. Little by little, Tommy seems to have overcome his initial anxiety. He abandoned his compulsive scribbling with the color brown and then got to the point of mixing colors, though he continued to paint in a state of arousal close to masturbatory compulsion. Unfortunately, we know nothing about the linguistic context in which this activity began and developed, but it was apparently within himself that Tommy found the resources with which to master his trauma.

According to Freud (1920), we are provided with a stimulus barrier against the external world, so that excitations, chiefly those of pleasure–unpleasure, reach us only in diminished form. In contrast, the internal system is not shielded in this way, and so internal stimuli are liable to produce an excessive amount of unpleasure. Thus we are tempted to displace internal unpleasure to the outside; this is, for Freud, the origin of the mechanism of projection. Early trauma is due to a failure of the protective system. In such cases, the psyche must master the excitation and undo it, but the psychic apparatus tends to cling to the available sources of pleasure and is reluctant to give them up in the face of the reality principle. It is at this very moment that the child sees an outlet in fantasy and play. Likewise, for Freud, art can reconcile the pleasure principle and the reality principle as the artist transforms the world through his creation.

Giving small children the opportunity to paint, to invent a world of their own making, is all the more important since, as with Tommy, this allows them to express what has hurt them in a language without words, even if they are unaware of what is inherent in their scribbles. The important thing is that their loneliness, their unhappiness, and their "craziness" can find expression, and can do so without an adult immediately seeking to supply a meaning. We must be wary of making sense, at all costs, out of nonsense, of rushing to establish facts prematurely (cf. Khan 1983).

Kris (1955) also describes a little girl, Evelyne, aged two and a half. One day in November, four weeks after she had familiarized herself with the paintbrushes, the colors, and the easel, she painted a large circle in which she placed two eyes, a nose, and a mouth, identifying this as a Halloween mask. Evelyne was an independent, brave

child, but several days before she started to paint she had
been terribly frightened by the Halloween masks worn
by the children. Now, in a need to separate herself or to
refind herself somehow, she was trying to reproduce the
way in which she had felt herself looked at by the masks.
As Lacan says, "From the moment this gaze exists, I am
already something other, in that I feel myself becoming
an object for the gaze of others. But in this position, which
is a reciprocal one, others also know that I am an object
who knows himself to be seen" (1953–1954, p. 215).

In the dialectic of the gaze, he continues, what counts
is that "the other sees . . . where I am not," because what
structures the relationship is "what is not there" (p. 224).
The painter, Lacan says elsewhere, presents in his painting something that "might be summed up thus—*You want
to see? Well, take a look at this!*" and invites the viewer "to
lay down his gaze there as one lays down one's weapons"
(1964, p. 101).

In painting the horror of an experience, Evelyne
herself put down her weapons, transposing to an Other
stage the hate and the fear of the violence that she perceived as coming from the other. As Melanie Klein (1948)
observes, the presence of a loving mother mitigates the
fear of the terrifying internal mother of the child's fantasies. Evelyne, confronted by the ghostly mask, felt
alone, but in reality she was waging a secret war against
the cleanliness imposed on her by her mother. Her reaction took the form of an aggressive niceness. As a little
girl, Evelyne's mother had waged a similar battle against

her own upbringing by a rigid mother. Kris' study, based on the work of Sally Provence, addresses the problem of intergenerational female identifications, and, to be sure, what we find in Evelyne's mother is the same intolerance, the same concern for a strict, conformist upbringing, that her own mother had shown. But we could, instead, follow Françoise Dolto (1981) in seeing culture at work here. What cradles the exchanges between the mother and her baby is the entire wordless language that conveys, through affect, notions of good and bad. The child builds an inner sense of safety on the presence and absence of the mother (or of the mother's mother): through her presence, the mother guarantees a familiar space.

Evelyne, like her mother, was independent and alert. Yet women who were "good" mothers to an infant may be less well suited to the raising of the child once he or she becomes independent. They may become phobic about the child's body (and the odors associated with the anal and urinogenital regions). Enuresis or encopresis in the child is experienced by these mothers as a narcissistic wound; their obsessive struggle for cleanliness is mingled with anxiety, and, quite often, His or Her Majesty the Baby usurps the position of the husband and the older siblings. It is then that the maternal line can refuse to identify the child with the women of the family. Their own childhood was damaged by the older generation of women, but nonetheless, when they themselves become mothers, they can replicate the anti-life behavior of their maternal tradition.

Evelyne had been brought up to be precocious. The author notes that she was given every possible educational toy, and, when she was seven months old, her mother had tried to get her to displace her masturbation onto the fantasy level. At nineteen months she began to play with imaginary companions and was well acquainted with all the Winnicottian fetish objects and transitional objects. Since her mother taught art, the child was introduced to painting early on. What proved to be important was not so much her talent as the ease with which she was able to use painting to transform the harm she had experienced, the anxiety and the underlying terror.

As a contrast to Evelyne's story, the author relates the case of Anne. This child's development had been troubled by the unconscious resentment of her mother, who had given up her career as an art teacher to raise her daughter. Between six and twelve months, the baby was like a child raised in an institution. Matters changed when Anne was one year old and her mother became her art teacher, as her own father had been for her. At the age of two and a half—the same age as Evelyne—Anne was noticeably anxious, but she was very alert and of above-average intelligence for her age. The mother was completely fulfilled by the child's verbal facility, and their shared interest in art was the bridge that eased Anne's entry into nursery school, where her attachment to her mother was transferred to her teachers. The mother, now pregnant, did not dare to speak of her condition to Anne. The little girl reacted by regressing in an area where she could attack her mother without endangering her too much: she did not become enuretic, but she deteriorated with regard to her verbal and intellectual achievements. Accordingly, her sublimation did not reach the same level of freedom and spontaneity that Evelyne was able to show.

When they appear early in life, aggression and anxiety affect the individual's development (cf. Klein 1948). If they cannot be expressed because the environment is unable to accept a destructive outburst, the result may be major inhibitions and neurotic suffering. On the other hand, Kris underscores Freud's emphasis on the baby's identification with the active mother and the later results of the ambivalent early exchange between the infant and the adult who carries him and provides what Winnicott (1958) calls holding and handling. When the baby sees the expression on his mother's face, he becomes aware of himself, of his own being. If the mother's gaze is empty, or if the mother-substitute is indifferent to the quality of the emotional exchanges, the baby can feel disorganized to the point of chaos. Abandoned or institutionalized babies are depressed and do not respond to stimulation. The child who is not "assisted" is thus readily inhabited by the death instinct (Dolto 1981) and finds it hard to achieve the symbolization of destructive experience. If the mother is dead or absent, the child will have to mourn the most archaic part of his history. Later, in adulthood (and sometimes well before then), he may fall prey to feelings of derealization, clinging nostalgically to the myth of an early childhood in which a woman was there to comfort his distress and his despair.

When Winnicott (1971) speaks of the "good enough" mother, he is pointing out that the child will not receive enough stimulation unless cared for by his mother. But, he adds, it is when the child passes from the illusion of being one with the mother to the disillusion of separateness that, using whatever aggressivity the environment allows him, he becomes able to find in himself the imaginary resources he will later put to work in creativity and sublimation. According to Freud (1929), it is difficult to speak of sublimation in this regard, because the young child's play and creativity are still too close to the aggressive drive and to the pleasure of satisfying what is still the "savage" part of the child, the part that has not yet been domesticated by the ego. Yet it is by obeying the pleasure principle that play begins to open the door to reality, bringing the individual the joy that allows him to overcome his troubles. It is, of course, also true that, in cases of pathology, play can foster a denial of reality, and this may take the form of refusing the presence of another person when the child is anxious to remain a prisoner of the rules he himself has set up.

# ——— 6 ———
# *The Symbolic Dimension of Play*

As Winnicott (1971) observes, creation is not the same thing as works of art. The creativity that interests Winnicott entails a certain *joie de vivre* and presupposes an inner world in which peace and war alternate. The apprehension of external reality, in the early months and years, draws on inner reality, be it terrifying or serene. It is in this intermediate space between the individual and his environment that the subject finds the wherewithal to construct his experience of life. This experience, in turn drawing on illusion and play, must be supported by a sense of safety, of trust in the other. When this is the case, the subject can express himself without fear that he will be flooded with persecutory elements, becoming incapable of an imaginative life or needing to hide everything that is authentic within himself. If he has to seek refuge in a false-self structure, he shows of himself only what he thinks the other expects of him; his inner life is then often limited to an omnipotent fantasizing, self-enclosed, opening out neither to dreams nor to imagination. But creative play partakes of life and dreams.

Shut off from communication with others, lodged in a retreat to the point of thwarting all personal development, the subject has trouble with speech: he lacks the words to say what is happening with his state of being. He may make language into a barrier or express himself in legalese. Lacan contrasts empty speech that simply churns around, saying nothing, with full speech, "speech which aims at, which forms, the truth such as it becomes established in the recognition of one person by another" (1953–1954, p. 107). Observing that illusion and opacity play a part in intersubjective experience, Lacan did not wish the analytic method to be identified with a game. For the aim of analysis is to give the subject access to full speech and thereby to a fuller authenticity, which can occur only through speech that has been loosened from its moorings. When the subject's speech is thus reworked in analysis, it becomes possible for him to recognize his desire.

Masud Khan (1983) takes up this dialectic in his contrast between speech (which he assimilates to the spoken word) and language (by which he means written language), reintroducing the notion of play as theorized by Winnicott and by Octave Mannoni. Khan explains how the human being is alienated from himself by the ability to speak; speech, originally intended for purposes of play, has become an instrument of tyranny. And it is to get out of this impasse, in which speech comes up against the wall of language, that Freud invented the play space of psychoanalysis. Play can be a playing with words that enables the patient to make the symptom speak (Lacan compares the symptom to knotted-up speech). The symptom, Khan reminds us, is a silent defensive strategy through which the subject protects himself from the all-powerful language of others. This is what Charcot's patients illustrated, and it took Freud to show that the symptom is a language that does not say what it is about.

The analyst must reconnect with the language of children, in which something is trying to be said and, at the same time, to slip away. Octave Mannoni (1980) makes his own distinction between language and speech. If the normal child achieves language use alone, he is no different from a child with elective mutism, who also possesses language but refuses to engage in speech. When children have only gestures by way of speech, we must listen closely to them and learn from them in order to translate into our words what they are trying to say. In the case of Victor, the wild boy of Aveyron (in Malson 1972), it is striking that it was Madame Guérin, the governess, and not Itard, the doctor, who was better able to guess the meanings of the syllables Victor uttered, such as the syllable *gli* that he pronounced in the Italian manner for *Julie*. It was with Madame Guérin that he developed a play space with words; Dr. Itard's a priori concepts about the nature of language merely prevented his patient from learning to speak. For the physician, words expressed a need, whereas Victor, the child, made a game between himself and words, as it pleased him.

Thus there has been a failure to understand the nature of the problem confronting the child before he learns signs. The child's first need is *to be seen* in a way that does not distort his being, so that he can then locate himself, recognizing his body in space and time, before he is ready to acquire any type of knowledge.

Octave Mannoni (1980, pp. 85–99) has reported two linguistic experiences from his childhood. In the first, when he was very young, it was raining, and the raindrops streaming on the window covered it with "upside-down exclamation points." He was fascinated and remained unusually still. He asked his mother, "What's that called?" "That's rain; it's water," she replied. But he was not satisfied and kept asking until, exasperated, she said, "It hasn't got a name." Throughout his childhood and even as an adult, he tried to learn the name for what had fascinated him at that moment. His hope was always disappointed, but he found photographers who were interested enough in the phenomenon to fix it on film!

The second experience concerned forbidden language. His parents thought they were teaching him French, but between themselves they used a private language, Corsican. Octave soon came to realize that his parents turned to this language when they wanted to speak about him or about matters that were none of his business. Corsican therefore became a forbidden language for him, and he was careful not to let his parents know that he understood them. "Can one be the subject of a language that one understands perfectly but never speaks?" he wondered later, recognizing that his experience was like that of an electively mute child. The difficulty for such a child is to engage in speech, and when he does so for the first time, he speaks to no one: speech is forbidden him insofar as it is the property of the other. Obviously, this is not just *any* other; speech is gotten from someone in order to be addressed to someone.

There are some families that, without being fully aware of it, forbid children language itself. And some young children are unable to say "I"; they will say, for example, "You've played enough now." It is almost impossible to change this through education, since what is at issue is the *place of the subject*. It is only when the child finally manages to find his place as subject that he can accept "I" as opposed to "you." The soil in which linguistic intelligence is rooted is that of the very first exchanges between the infant and his mother. Such play, Winnicott (1951) insists, is also found in the choice of words, the speech patterns and inflections, even the use of humor, in the psychoanalytic situation.

Françoise Dolto (1981) has described a peek-a-boo game similar to the *fort/da* that Freud (1920) identified as the origin of language. In a public garden one day, she met a nine-month-old baby boy being wheeled in a car-

riage by a mother who described the child as unruly and
developmentally delayed. To amuse the child, Dolto gave
him her hat, which he had been looking at, and named
it "Hat." The child would not touch it. Dolto held it up
and repeated, "Hat," then placed it on the carriage cover.
The child reached out and touched it, and slowly a game
unfolded. Dolto took the baby's hands and placed them
on the hat, saying, "The lady's hat." She put the hat back
on her head; the child held out his arms; Dolto held out
the hat once again; the child happily grabbed it. With
each movement, Dolto said, "Pretty hat!" Finally the baby,
excited, took the hat and threw it out of the carriage. The
mother then intervened to say that she hadn't given the
hat to the baby because the child was so fond of throwing things. What gave the child pleasure was getting rid
of things and then triumphantly recovering them, but the
mother wanted no part of this.

The game of "hat/no more hat" continued between
Dolto and the happy child. But Dolto noticed that what
most interested the baby was the *naming*, to the point
where they could even play at complicity in a lie, when
the word did not correspond to the gesture and Dolto
said "hat" when the hat was not there. This kind of game
helps a baby to win mastery and independence. In the
present case, we can see how a preventive move on Dolto's
part helped the mother to do right by her child: the baby's
listlessness and his lack of zest, of interest in the outer
world, stemmed from a relationship with his mother that
left him no place as a subject, since what was wanted of

him was that he should forget himself so as not to be a nuisance.

The game with the spool described by Freud (1920), like Dolto's hat game, is important not so much because the object is conserved despite being discarded, as because the object is supported by language, the source of symbolic mastery.

Octave Mannoni (1980) stresses the difference between the Winnicottian object that fills the gap left by absence and the Freudian object that opens out onto the *Witz*, the joke. While Freud tried to give a rational explanation for play on the basis of the joke, for Winnicott rational thought itself is derived from play. These different positions suggest two contrasting pedagogical approaches: either teachers use achievement-oriented techniques to promote an increasing adaptation to reality, or they listen to the nonsense of desire. Now, Octave Mannoni continues, we have no guarantee that the world will reject a frenzied pursuit of adaptation; if it does not do so, there will be only one universe of false selves (including analysts) congratulating themselves and one another.

At Bonneuil (see Chapter 7), twenty years ago, we met a teacher of disturbed children who were diagnosed as mentally ill. He sent us a tape of the sounds of the town, Graniès, in which he worked. "His" children sang and talked about their daily activities, and then a voice began to *name* the children of Bonneuil, one by one. The effect of this was truly one of shock: children who had been electively mute for four years were overwhelmed with joy. And the rest of the tape was listened to in a religious silence.

Then it was our turn to speak into the tape and send a message to the children of Graniès. The speech of some of the children was choked up; their emotion was such that their tears spoke what could not be said in words. Others, in contrast, poured out a stream of empty, conventional talk, saying, in effect, that the absent listener should remain absent so that they themselves could go back to daydreaming. The electively mute children sang and played with sounds; one of them began to call his mother (but, surely, so that she would not come), calling her as if echoing the cowbells, the noise coming from that other place we had been talking about.

With these children who have been diagnosed as autistic, psychotic, or retarded, everything has to be reinvented continually. From a place where death and life are closely linked, an element of choice arises that challenges us at a deep level. For what is required of us, in our journey with these children, is that we undo our own defenses. This is why they sometimes leave us totally exhausted, and it is also why any institution dedicated to the care of such children, however innovative it may have been at its founding, cannot stay attuned to these children unless the team is renewed by the presence of enough trainees coming from without and asking questions from different perspectives. If this is not the case, sclerosis, paralysis, and routine will quickly take over, for this is the way the adults can protect themselves from their ultra-sensitive charges.

Speech begins to circulate once it is located in a register beyond the imaginary other. For the children I have just described, the message that came from such an "elsewhere" took on meaning after the fact. "On the level of the unconscious," Lacan says, "he [the child] does not know what he is. And then he finds himself caught up in language and receiving from the other the sign (*signum*) of his relation with the other . . . . Even if the child cannot yet carry on a conversation, he already knows how to speak."[1] Lacan goes on to explain that "he already knows how to speak" means that there is something for the child beyond the captivity in language: there is a relation, insofar as there is an appeal from the other as a presence against the background of absence.

Resistance to putting feelings into words occurs, Lacan says,

> at the moment when the speech of revelation is not said, . . . when the subject can no longer manage. He hooks onto the other because what is pressing toward speech hasn't attained it. The blocked arrival of speech, insofar as something perhaps renders it fundamentally impossible, is the pivotal point around which, in analysis, speech tips all the way over into

---

1. Personal notes taken at Lacan's seminar of November 12, 1958; cf. Lacan 1958–1959.

its initial aspect and is reduced to its function of relationship to the other. If speech then functions as
mediation, it is because it has not been achieved as
revelation. [1953–1954, p. 49, translation modified]

Resistance, he reminds us, "is embodied in the system of
the ego and the other" (p. 50).

And this brings us back to the hat game with the "list-
less" baby that I mentioned earlier in this chapter. An area
of play is necessary between the subject and the other so
that the imagination can be accepted and the subject can
take up speech. Speech is taken up in relation to someone, and, as Octave Mannoni says, "we never ask who this
someone is" (1980, p. 95). But a subject can have a per-
fect command of a language without feeling entitled to
use it.

# 7

## *The Birth of the Institution: Meeting Artaud and Grotowski*

## The Beginnings

When we created the experimental school at Bonneuil in 1969,[1] we had a dozen troubled children, aged five to thirteen, almost all of whom had major mental illness. The team, whose members were all on a volunteer basis until 1975, was led by interns and especially by students from the University of Paris VII, students of Pierre Fedida. They came because we offered them a clinical adventure outside the mainstream, and so we had to start from scratch. Weekly meetings with the analysts Robert Lefort

---

1. For a fuller discussion, see M. Mannoni 1973, pp. 158–198.

and Pierre Fedida were aimed at keeping an open mind so as not to fall into a routine.

When we asked ourselves about the institutional framework we wanted to establish, we found that we had to set up minimal guidelines. For example, we quickly noticed that the children were disturbed when adults left a studio. We therefore affirmed the concept of the permanence of a studio and its functioning, even though one of its main organizers might not be present. Whether we wanted to or not, we had to ensure the existence of a permanent frame within which free creative expression could take place, a frame that reflects the way human beings deal with aggressivity. If the frame is not maintained, the patient finds himself alone in his fantasy world, and when he suddenly loses the container for his anxiety, he acts out. Thus, when a workshop was canceled because the adults could not coordinate their plans, this non-place was felt by the children as an abdication of responsibility.

We gradually began to realize that, if we had to guarantee the continuity of the studios in time, we also had to make sure that there was a modicum of respect for the instruments used in painting, music, and so forth. Once this minimal guarantee was imposed, we witnessed an explosion of creative freedom. In each studio, the session opened with a mythic ritual serving to bring the children together. What they did after that was up to them. Speech can arise from a field of language, but not from a cacophony.

The unconscious shows that, as Lacan[2] so often emphasized, desire depends on prohibition: it is the acceptance of one's "castration" that creates the lack opening out onto desire. When we state the problematics of desire, we are at the same time postulating the relation of desire to the Law. For, right from the outset, the child seeking pleasure in the other encounters a constraint that is both necessary and fundamental, and this constraint is what makes it possible for him to separate from the fascinating capture by his narcissistic double and to constitute himself as an other outside the lethal clash with the sameness of that double.

From birth on, the child is confronted with checks on his wishes. The restrictions imposed by childrearing practices, varying from one culture to another, have transformative effects that orient desire and the possibilities for its realization. This mark left by the inevitable changes accompanying each stage of life is what is called *castration* in Lacanian analytic jargon. As we shall see, this castration has what Françoise Dolto (1981, p. 302) called a symbol-generating value.

The question of the relation between the sexes arose when our patients' fathers raised concerns about their

2. Translator's note: For a brief introduction to Lacanian thought and the Lacanian terms Maud Mannoni will be using (symbolic, imaginary, real, castration, desire, other/Other, etc.) see Gurewich and Tort, in press, pp. 1–34; more detailed theoretical explanations can be found in Dor 1998.

daughters. To formulate the matter in the terms of Lévi-Strauss (1949), these fathers presented the problem of withholding their daughters from circulation, from exchange. It was in these terms of exchange that the problem was discussed with the boys: a man receives a woman from another man; if one day he has a daughter with this woman, he must accept in turn the need to give her to another man, outside the group, later on. We therefore agreed that the children comprising the Bonneuil group could not be allowed to "hit on" each other, but they were free to find a boyfriend or girlfriend outside Bonneuil.

Formulating the problem of sexual prohibition in terms of the Name of the Father and the chain of symbolic exchanges on which a society is founded[3] made it clear that what was at stake was bound up with the Oedipus complex and castration. In this context, the arbitrariness of the prohibition was no more and no less than a structural requirement, but this became apparent only later.

"It's artificial, that gimmick," one teenager told us. "It's as though we were all named Bonneuil, and that's why we can't come on to people in the same family." The theoretical justification can seem to be a "gimmick" de-

---

3. Translator's note: The Name (*Nom*) of the Father is also his "No" (*Non*), his prohibition of incest. For the influence of Lévi-Strauss on Lacan's theories of the symbolic father, the incest taboo, and the child's entry into language, see Gurewich and Tort, in press, pp. 13–18.

signed to maintain the established order. But this is by no means the case. What we came to realize in actual practice was that a law (the prohibition), formulated in its relation to the circuit of exchange, brought to the surface everything that, on various levels of functioning, was at an impasse in the school. It is when things become immobilized, on the level of exchange, that neither the child nor the adult can continue speaking, for then death sets in, and the door is opened to the institutionalization of madness.

Thus our first theoretical references were structural ones: it is around certain laws (prohibition of exploitation, of incest) that human order—that is, a symbolic order—is established and that the child, caught up in this signifying machine, comes to find personal speech and to locate himself differently with regard to his desire and to the desire of the other.

I shall be taking up this question again further on, in connection with examples from our experience at the school. For now, I want to describe how, learning from attempts oriented more toward listening to children than to the collective, we tried to give birth to an institution, that is, to the work accomplished by the children themselves, who gradually, along with the adults, became the guardians of the (few) rules set forth so that there could be a communal life. In the state of grace that accompanied the beginning of our experiment, we created a Cooperative Council; this Council arranged the program for the day, chose the people responsible for various activities, and (until governmental policy affected the economics of the school) taught the children to manage a budget for the food that we bought together with them.

Life at Bonneuil is organized around two axes. The kitchen is always a convivial place that proves essential to children in crisis, a place where guests from outside can carry on fruitful exchanges with the adults in the institution. The other axis is contact with the outside world, exchanges with other children, other schools, and other countries through painting, putting out a newspaper, and taping messages so as not to restrict the children to writing. Although governmental policies eventually curtailed some of these activities, each child gets to know a variety of host families, artisans, and peasants in the area of Bonneuil.

Alongside these basic activities, there is the children's education, which takes place through correspondence courses. In this way, the teacher who corrects and annotates their work is "elsewhere," and the adults at Bonneuil are there as companions to ease the enormous difficulties some of these children have. The educational dimension is an opening to the world, since at least one morning a week and sometimes more, the children are taken to the workshop of a craftsman or artisan. This other discourse in which the young child is involved, and the companionship of the older children who welcome him, is especially effective in clearing up certain learning inhibitions. In some cases, for example, a mechanic will tell the educator, in the child's presence, "Right now he can't go any further unless he knows more math." The child is imbued with the *desire* to learn a particular way of doing things, or to get his diploma, or simply to take part in life more fully.

The morning begins with Chat Time, bringing the children together in groups at different levels. They talk about their house, their projects, their problems. The adults set out the schedule for the day: schoolwork (intensive for some), always alternating with other activities; outside work; studio time for creative work. Before Bonneuil received accreditation and had to conform to state guidelines, there were also meetings, presided over by the children, at which relations within Bonneuil and with the outside community were discussed. One child had been questioned by the police, for example, or certain activities had harmed the reputation of the school or violated its internal rules. These meetings were friendly enough to bind the children together in defending standards and enabled them to lead a normal life in the town. They served to articulate symbolically everything that had been stuck in the complaints and demands belonging to the imaginary level. Thus we analyzed the idea of *obligation*: the obligation to live and let live, the obligation to give and receive in the order of exchange. Here we came up against the group unconscious as well as the individual unconscious, including the pressure sometimes exerted by a threatening and devastating superego. It is this unconscious law of the group that structures what we are establishing.

In tending to the exchange of information—about construction projects and runaway children alike—the institution combats death. We therefore continually refer to what is happening on the outside. Though the format of the meetings has changed, what remains in place is the concept of the "exploded institution" (M. Mannoni 1973),[4] in which the children of Bonneuil maintain interest in what is going on with one or the other of them in the outside world. Visits from "alumni" of the school are eagerly awaited. One such person may have become a computer specialist who earns more than our institute psychologist; another tells us about his responsibilities as a financial officer; another describes his life with "his" goats.

The other activities are centered in the studios: painting, theater, music, storytelling, pottery, sculpture, and expressive movement, among others. The creative life of the school has thrived, and we have given theatrical performances locally and in Paris and also held art exhibitions and craft sales. I shall describe later on how, in this endeavor, we were "reshuffled" by Antonin Artaud and Jerzy Grotowski.

---

4. Translator's note: "exploded" here has the meaning of an "exploded view," one in which different perspectives and levels of a complex structure can be seen.

We were particularly concerned to make electively mute autistic children aware that they could learn to say with their bodies what could not be said in words, to make the body a welcoming and familiar place in which to dwell and not an object experienced as alien. This form of communication brought into play not only rhythm but also the special relation that the child establishes with clay from the time when he allows himself to have hands. We may create alone or create collectively, but we are more willing to create if we have the right to refuse. What cannot be said with clay can sometimes be said through painting or music. An extensive range of artistic activities was thus maintained over the years.

The importance accorded to the child's speech in a collective prevents the institution from becoming rigid. It is always, or almost always, through something negative that something of the nature of *true speech* can be expressed. The patient spontaneously offers resistance to change, as if seeking firm boundaries to control the part of himself that feels endangered by the dynamism and movement of a changing world. The framework of institutional activities is the repository of the patient's fantasmatic world and must become the object of analysis in order to undo the patient's psychotic bonds with the institution. The inertia of the institutional framework protects against anxiety. The adults must be able to sustain the children's question, "What do you want from me?" For it is here that the child often becomes entrapped in his relations with others.

The regular meetings chaired by the children ceased at a time when the attention of the staff was focused on new creative resources, increased attention to scholastic matters, and a search for craftspeople and work opportunities in the surrounding area that would guarantee for those who could not return to "normal" life a direction suitable to their unique natures and a place in which they could live and work, at their own pace, with a positive quality of life. The meetings could have continued if they had been compatible with what was taking place in other areas at Bonneuil. Once the school was accredited by the government in 1975 and no longer had to rely on a largely voluntary staff, many parents wanted an "upscale" alternative to traditional institutionalization, but, over the years, there was a general decrease in the militant demand for social policies benefiting the mentally ill. In 1969, the signifier "Maud Mannoni" made me the object of a massive transference. In 1975, this switched to the signifier "Bonneuil," and the school became the subject of books and films. The transference then moved onto the team (and it is an excellent one), but in an institutional perspective that is large-scale and anonymous.

To make room once again for the child's speech and to safeguard a space for analytic listening, we had to reintroduce myths and not only rethink our approach to creativity, but, with the wordless child, reinvent a different relation to his body. It became possible to give language to every form of desiring production.

## The Theater

In looking for a way to bring mentally ill children onto the stage from the perspective of the theater of the unconscious (cf. Bouquier and Richer 1976), we found our inspiration in Artaud and Grotowski. We had to avoid imprisoning the children in roles, and we had to see to it that there arose the need for speech unfettered by stereotypes, while also enabling the mute children to have a physical presence on the stage. Grotowski (1968) began by trying to establish for each child a wide variety of physical exercises adapted to the personality of the future actor. His idea of training was doing away with the inhibitions of a body in which the actor must learn to dwell. The actor must learn to decode whatever he can perceive from his body: on the respiratory level (since there are different kinds of breathing), in the voice (which comes from the mouth, the stomach, the chest, the head, the larynx, the nose), and so forth. It is not enough for the actor to try out different ways of breathing; he has to be able to choose a certain kind *unconsciously,* to reveal himself and become more and more true.

Grotowski is thus thinking in terms of a "total theater," a theater that brings the body, and its inhibitions, into play. In the course of the exercises that he practiced with his pupils—in a progressive order, with one, then two, three, four, and so on—he would also ask them to be, for example, a tiger attacking its prey. The point was not just to roar, but to understand with which bodily source of sound roaring is produced. Other exercises consisted of singing "la, la, la," with Grotowski lying down next to the child and repeating "la, la, la" toward the ceiling, then toward the wall and toward the floor, then massaging his stomach in order, as he said, to untie and stimulate the resonance inside it. The children imitated the meowing of a cat, the hissing of a snake, the mooing of a cow. Together with Ryszard Cieslak, Grotowski set as a theme for improvisation a cat waking up and stretching, and through such exercises the children became aware of how their bodies adapted to each movement. Cieslak introduced still other physical exercises: miming the relaxation of a tired spinal column, or reproducing the echo that comes from the ground when a cow moos. Finally, there were exercises that enabled the fingers to become differentiated from the hand, games with toes, and the like.

This was not gymnastics but rather the expression of a living process that had been blocked by causes foreign to the function of one or the other body part. In her book *Le corps a ses raisons* [*The Body has its Reasons*], Thérèse Bertherat (1976) explains how these "anti-gymnastic" exercises lead the body to give up its old habits. The body has taken fright, she says, and fear of the body and fear of words sometimes go together. Someone who knows his body refuses only what is false for him, what he does not experience in his body. As Grotowski (1968) says, we have to find the resistances, find what is blocking the person in his breathing, his movement, and—most important—in human contacts.

We were fortunate to have on our team a professional actress who had become an analyst. Far from trying to "train actors" by following Grotowski's guidelines to the letter, she helped us remain attuned to the language of the autistic child's body, that wordless language of which Freud first showed us living examples.

For Margaret Mahler (1968), our bodily sensations are the source of our growing feeling of individual identity and separation from the object. The baby is at first attentive to the internal processes that take place inside it during feeding and holding; perception at a distance comes later. It is the interaction of the two processes that, for Mahler, gives rise to the *body schema*, that is, a representation of one's own body that constitutes the nucleus of the self. If the first process—registering the impressions from direct contact—impedes perception at a distance, a stable body schema cannot develop.

This schema, however, does not coincide with the objective body. In the course of the first year, the differentiation of the body ego is achieved and, as Winnicott (1951) showed with regard to the transitional object as the first "not-me" possession, it becomes possible for the subject to separate from the object. The "I" emerges along with locomotion, and it is then that the child may become anxious, sometimes to the point of desperately denying separation at the same time as he struggles against the fear of re-engulfment by the adult. The child who cannot function apart from his symbiotic partner returns to the delusional fantasy of unity with the omnipotent mother, of being an extension of her body.

It is not the real loss of the object that leads to the psychotic break with reality; the origin of psychotic disturbance must be sought in difficulties with the earliest mother–child interactions. Mahler (1968) emphasizes the distinction between autism as a syndrome and autistic-like retreat as a temporary defense. According to her, there is a difference between a rigid autism marked by loss of a sense of life and, on the other hand, a temporary regression in the service of what Winnicott (1951) calls "the perpetual human task of keeping inner and outer reality separate yet inter-related" (p. 23). Although Winnicott (1949) admits that "it is logical . . . to oppose the emotional development and the bodily development of an individual," he maintains that "[m]ental phenomena are complications of variable importance in psyche-soma continuity of being, in that which adds up to the individual's 'self'" (p. 254).

The body in analysis is the body of which one speaks. But, in the approaches to play at Bonneuil, listening to the "blocked body" of the autistic child is of great importance. Such a child becomes present in the world, in a wordless language, as soon as he can overcome his fears regarding his own body, which, until that time, had seemed to him like a strange body that did not belong to him. A dialectic becomes possible as soon as he can begin to inhabit his body and make it speak to him in its language.

Grotowski (1968) observes that, for him, the important thing is not words but what we do with them, the way actors give life to the inanimate words of a script. For Artaud (1967), the theater is mobile, and the actor does not repeat the same gesture twice. Artaud's is a theater that makes use of all the languages: gestures, sounds, words, and cries, going far beyond the written words of the script. Inspired by these ideas, the adults at Bonneuil created their own interpretation of (among other works) *Alice in Wonderland,* in which the children became the authors of tableaux vivants (M. Mannoni 1976). But this was possible only after extensive preparation, during which time we had to make a detour through a "spoken body" in order to free it from the terror that enclosed it. The force of a great work, Grotowski tells us, is to open doors that lead to self-transcendence, so that we can find what is hidden inside us and accomplish the act of encountering other people.

The children grasped the outlines of stories that, on the unconscious level, called out to them. Freed from the script, they were able, in their own language and with different words each time, to send a message to the audience. In addition, the words exchanged onstage between them and the adults re-established something of a communication that had been lost. The theater was the "container" in which playing occurred. This place, far from being one in which madness was unleashed, imposed upon the actors the most rigorous conventions.

When a boy, caught up in words that abruptly brought him back to his anxiety, forgot that he was on a stage and banged into the scenery in an attempt to escape, shouting, "I'm scared, let me leave," the adults echoed, "Alice wants to leave. She's scared. It's dark" (M. Mannoni 1976, pp. 168–175). The child, astonished, replied, "I want to leave. Armand wants to leave; Alice wants to leave; I'm scared." In a quite amazing way this boy, by expressing distress that was heard and understood, managed to put himself in the skin of the character he was playing. Now it was from the place of Alice that he spoke of his anxiety, anxiety that, suddenly, was not entirely his own. He could play Alice within theatrical conventions, overcoming his terror by displacing it onto the terror that a little girl, Alice, had experienced long ago in the past.

Bouquier and Richer (1976) emphasize the clinical reality of what Freud says "when he proposes that it is to the extent that the subjective drama is integrated into a myth having a widespread, even a universal, human value that the subject brings himself into being" (p. 170, citing Lacan 1953–1954, p. 191). This boy, the authors add, "was able to achieve a symbolization that, before, had been impossible or absent." He was able to transpose a threatening bit of the real into the imaginary of theatrical playing, and, at the same time, to disidentify from the part of himself that was terrified—so much so that, one day, he said to us, "I'm playing at being scary and at scaring myself." The opposite might have been the case in the kind of playing in which the actor has to "stick to the script" and "sticks" to it so well that he remains, in his "real life," a prisoner of the role. In such cases, Octave Mannoni (1969) tells us, the role "could not be confined to its proper function, which was to show an imaginary character. We cannot tell whether the actor considered life to be imaginary or the theater to be real" (p. 305).

Bouquier and Richer report that the adults were left exhausted and drained by certain performances in which they had to go back to the symptom while respecting theatrical conventions. The play was put on in a theater before a real audience, and, each time, the adults were afraid that the performance might turn into a "happening" of madness. Bouquier and Richer mention another performance in the course of which Armand, forgetting that he was playing Alice, cried, "I want to go away!" "Silence," answered the king, "or I'll clear the court." "Oh, O.K.," replied Armand, who once more took up his role in the play. The authors also mention scenes in which wordplay proliferated to the point where the audience wondered whether all the replies were intended or not.

Even if the theater involves an effect of illusion for the audience, it offers the actor the potential for symbolization, thanks to a form of playing in which imaginary and real are not confused. A genuine theatrical work frees up the imagination, writes Artaud (1967). Like the plague, it makes the mask fall. This is not the decadent idea of a work of art as a charming pastime, Artaud insists, but of art that invites us to react insofar as we are all mad, desperate, and sick.

Once the theater is no longer subjected to the script, actor and audience alike can reconnect with the unconscious, that is, with the element of madness and childhood—of truth—that persists in each of us. As Grotowski says, nothing touches the unconscious of the spectator and the actor better than myths. And indeed, myths convey everything that, from the beginning of time, relates to birth, death, love, and cruelty. We have to tear ourselves away from a script in order to make its truth spring forth. In so doing, we restore a truth on the unconscious level that was hiding behind the stereotypy of lines to be repeated word for word. These mythical themes are the ones that have to be brought to life.

The lesson to be learned from Antonin Artaud is his illness: how he made use of an Other stage to project his distress, his violence, his rebellion, his hatred for a civilization that he described as sick. With a sincerity that touches each of us, he transformed what Grotowski calls his violence and inner chaos into a truth. Artaud saw in the "total theater" of which he dreamed a form of therapy. He stressed, however, that in order to stage anarchy and chaos, one has to respect theatrical conventions. Cruelty, he said, is rigor.

Children who are "different," Bouquier and Richer note, bring a message of protest and dissent to adults who remain hopelessly deaf to the utterance of a disturbing truth. The theatrical work we did with these children shows that they can bring forth speech, with its meaning effects, that an audience will remember for a long time. (It may be mentioned here as an aside that the money brought in by the performances was handled by the children of Bonneuil, who decided on what things to buy for themselves.)

This theatrical experience allows the adults to reconnect with the madness and solitude of childhood in themselves. In the earliest period of life, the child learns to be alone in the presence of a reassuring adult. As he grows up, he achieves independence and becomes a person, but, as Khan (1983) points out, this aspect of infancy falls into oblivion. Nonetheless, the element of madness and solitude can be expressed in art, literature, the theater, and other forms of creativity. In analysis, patients sometimes reproduce in the session this need to be cut off from the world, and the analyst often interprets this silence as a resistance. If the analyst is bent on making sense of nonsense by reconstructing childhood events or fantasies, as Khan observes, he misses the creative potential of madness; these possibilities are once more forgotten, and the patient, no longer crazy and needing to be left in solitude, is just lost, abandoned.

At Bonneuil we try to remain attuned to this solitude, so that we can allow the speech that precedes words to find its interpreter and its expression.

## Storytelling

The storytelling workshop at Bonneuil got underway right from the beginning with an African woman who was a student of Pierre Fedida. The children gathered in a circle, with modeling clay in their hands, and listened:

> I'm going to tell you the stories of my childhood, as the griot[5] from my village handed them down to me. From generation to generation, the same stories were told, sometimes accompanied by songs and the rhythmic beat of the drum. Every night the audience was filled with fear and merriment. The griot of my village told us wondrous things. I can't do such a good job, but I'll be thinking of him as I tell you the stories of the turtle, the leopard lady, and the cannibal king, and also the stories that were sung about the misfortunes of Khary Gaye, the judgment of Madi-Katé-Kala, and the adventures of Golo the monkey.

These stories touched the children deep inside, since what they were listening to was the dramatization of their daily experience of passion, madness, and dreams.

---

5. A griot is a traditional African storyteller, the repository of the oral tradition. For the stories, see Raponda-Walker 1967 and Diop 1967.

At the time of her own marriage, the storyteller told the tale of "The little husband" (in Diop 1967). Why did she unconsciously choose this theme? In the middle of the story, she began to cry, and the children, moved, joined the adults in taking up the song:

> I say it and say it again,
> Little husband, little husband!

And the storyteller answered with the refrain:

> May your sister not send you away,
> N'Diongan, come back!

and continued the story at the point where she had stopped: "The little husband didn't answer; he had disappeared into the sea."

Now, the "little husband" was Khary's only brother, who she had determined would be her husband, after her father died, in order to help her mother emerge from her endless mourning. N'Diongan, she said to the mother, will be "our little husband." But the brother would have none of this and refused to be addressed in this way. After the circumcision ceremony that initiated him into manhood, he demanded that his mother make his sister stop viewing him as her potential husband. But the sister did not give up: her brother was the handsomest boy in the village and had to agree to marry her.

N'Diongan was firm: "Khary, tell your mother that I'm not coming home; I'm going away and will never come back." And he went away toward the sea. The mother's song calling to her son to return was joined by the sister's song, and the wind brought the boy's words back to them: "Mother, tell Khary not to call me 'little husband.'" But the sister stubbornly continued her lament:

> Little husband, little husband!
> I say it and say it again.

N'Diongan did not answer but disappeared into the sea forever. Then Kumba, the mother, grabbed Khary by the throat and buried first her head and then her body in the wet sand. Waves swept in and engulfed the daughter and Kumba, who continued to sing. "And," the storyteller concluded, "if you walk on the shore in the evening and put your ear to a seashell, what you hear are the weeping and the song of crazy Kumba calling her son:

> N'Diongan, come back,
> N'Diongan, dear, come back!

Freud (1912–1913), citing the anthropologist Northcote W. Thomas, explains the various purposes of the taboo, which include the warding off of trouble that may accompany major acts and rites of passage: birth, male initiation, marriage, sexual functions, and the like. There are permanent taboos on priests and chiefs, as well as on the dead and everything associated with them. Freud explains that primitive peoples have an ambivalent attitude toward their taboos, since they unconsciously wish to violate the prohibitions. The man who has violated a taboo arouses envy and, with his bad example, becomes a source of contagion.

In the story of "The little husband," the symbolic relation to the *dead father* (cf. Rosolato 1969) has disappeared, since the mother does not object to her daughter's infringing the prohibition of which the brother reminds her. The brother serves for both women as an idealized father: there has to be a man in the house, and this will be the brother, whom the girl imagines as her potential husband. But the reference to the dead father, the guarantor of the Law and its prohibitions, the axis of orientation for all generations, no longer exists. And therefore, as Rosolato points out, the death drive causes desire to overstep the bounds of the symbolic, and fantasies of hatred and destruction, as described by Melanie Klein (1948), along with their retaliatory effects, become points of fixation and regression for the psychoses. Death and sexuality, he says, are linked by castration, and sacrifice represents the mythic memory of this path to the symbolic.

What are the implications for the psychoanalyst of the taboo associated with the totemic system? As Freud (1912–1913) observes, the taboo involves the law of exogamy, the law forbidding sexual relations and marriage among members of a given totem group.

The tales of black Africans present greed, ingratitude, and lying, the anarchic forces that are opposed to order in life. References to cruel myths about the body, sex, and death create a situation in which the body of the participants sometimes takes part in the conversation, in accord with the Freudian metaphor for the symptom. When the storyteller burst into tears in the middle of the story of "The little husband," one of the girls in the group went into an epileptic dissociation, thereby echoing that which, in the adult, could not be symbolized. And the adult, confronted by what had escaped her, found her truth in the child's symptom.

At Bonneuil, each workshop has its ritual, and the African stories were told with ritual respect, evoking the village griot and the oral heritage. This ritual served as a symbolic frame of reference, in such a way that the child would not feel attacked by the "crazy stories" coming from the "imaginary" of the adult. When the transmission of the story failed, it was because one or the other remained trapped in imaginary fascination with death and violence.

There is always a complicity between discourse and what it casts off into "somewhere else." It is this rejected material that is important, because the field of speech is that of desire. Myth comes from nowhere, that is, from the unconscious—one might say from the ancestral unconscious. The message it sends has its effects on the level of the body, proof that language is reality. Myth always takes place at the origin, and we come up against an imaginary bounded by death and absence. Freud (1912–1913) asserts that myths are not commemorations of actual events; they are expressions of a wish for disorder, symbolic satisfactions of forbidden incest. Human beings always seek the world before the fall—hence the importance of handing down myths (or stories with a similar value) that are in touch with tradition and raise a fundamental issue in a signifying framework.

Allowing the children to handle modeling clay while listening to the stories enabled them to take out any aggression on the clay, so that they would not feel that they were being force-fed. The story evokes an image that then disappears but leaves a trace in the body (Pierre Fedida, personal communication): the unfolding of the plot creates a scene and then makes it disappear in the very moment it is experienced. This is why children react so intensely to stories. As they listen, they become actors in the narrative, and what the narrative deposits in them is reflected in bodily activity.

As Pierre Fedida has pointed out, stories—which our culture has impoverished—have a meaning in which sexuality is present and absent at the same time. What we see in African stories is the possibility of holding onto shit and molding it, kneading it. This encourages poetic, creative reworking. The tale transmits a secret that is terrible, horrible. As I listen, what I experience as dreadful takes me back to what remains of my own infantile amnesia. The dread aroused by the stories—whether the cruelty is emphasized or the violence toned down—is a sort of *event* that, for the child in his bodily experience, can be the equivalent of a sacrifice.

The problem of the relation to knowledge and truth was discussed in a work group led by Lacan:

> At the moment when the demand for knowledge is satisfied, desire is confronted by the truth of knowing—what is known is lost to desire. It is the aspect of desire with which [the subject] will always fail to become acquainted, which will always be excluded from the field of knowledge and will guarantee the resurgence of desire and the permanence of the status of the desirer. It is this that the knowledge of the Father speaks forth when the agency of the Law is brought to bear and forbids the subject from carnal knowledge of the mother. [Personal notes]

I feel that it is important to recall how, in the first flush of our beginnings and in each workshop—especially this one—the leader took part in the stories he chose to bring in. In this case the narrator was personally affected by a message from within the tale, and it was this to which the children responded. We need to attend to the *entire* range of effects produced by a narrative.

## Painting

Claude Halmos (in M. Mannoni 1976, pp 105–116) has discussed the framework we established to make a certain kind of painting possible. Here I would like to take a different tack, using the raw material Halmos presents in order to trace the path that led the participants in this studio to be "true painters," creating what Artaud (1967) calls a *scene*, a concrete physical place that asks to be filled and to speak its own concrete language. Artaud is referring to everything that can be said independently of words, a kind of poetry that appeals to the senses. He criticizes the notion of an art that aims only at delighting us in our spare time, for, as he says, life is not on one side, art on the other. Ordinary life is disrupted; despair and madness become a matter of concern to all. And Peter Brook (1968) warns the artist to keep on renewing himself so as not to become rigid. Pianists, dancers, and painters, he says, must put their art in question every day if it is not to decline.

This process of putting oneself in question in relation to the other is the context of the analyst's work and must not be lost sight of. For it would be dangerous and mistaken to retain from the published accounts of Bonneuil only what concerns the rigor of the frame and the rituals. To do so would be to forget that "it is to the extent that the subjective drama is integrated into a myth having a widespread, even a universal, human value that the subject brings himself into being" (Lacan 1953–1954, p. 191, translation modified). It is the style of a pursuit that must draw our attention if we are not to overlook possibilities of new discovery.

Lacan continues: infantile neurosis is tantamount to psychoanalysis. Between the ages of three and four, the subject learns to integrate the events of his life into a law, a field of symbolic meanings. The first symbolic integration can, on the imaginary level, come to have the import of a trauma, in that it exerts a repressive force retroactively. Thereafter the subject is "spoken" by something over which he has no control, and this, Lacan says, forms the nucleus of what will later be called his symptoms. What differentiates animal society from human society is the intersubjective dimension in the latter (Lacan 1953–1954, p. 240). And, in any analysis of the intersubjective relation, *what is most important is what is not there*, "it is only with speech that there are things which are—which are true or false, that is to say which are—and things which are not." But it is with speech that lying comes into being: "There is neither true nor false prior to speech" (p. 228).

At the end of an analysis, Lacan observes, what falls away is "the accidental, the trauma, the hitches of history. *And it is being which then comes to be constituted*" (p. 232, italics in original).

The adventure that unfolds in the workshops is not, strictly speaking, an analytic adventure. But the way in which each of the actors, child or adult, is engaged in an intersubjective relation, the effects of a dialectical reworking, are far from negligible. The adult still has to be able to understand the speech bound up in the symptom and must not get rid of the subject, and the discomfort that the subject causes, in the name-of-Lacan's-law, that plague of institutions. In becoming police officers, we are doing something quite contrary to what Lacan intended. We can use a "gimmick" of his, and another "gimmick" from Dolto, but then, just like the psychotic child, we are in the situation of being spoken, with no control over what is "doing us," motivating us to act this way. "You can get hit with speech," as one child said. The group leaders must avoid falling into this trap of the completely illusory aggressor–victim dyad.

Putting the children in a situation where they could be true painters, with a painter's materials, not to mention the restrictions involved in mixing colors and cleaning brushes, made possible the expression, the projection (on paper placed on the floor or pinned onto the wall) of latent disorder, dormant conflicts, all the violence and hate held in and unusable in real life but waiting to burst forth on an Other stage, freeing the unconscious. Of course, as we showed in the case of the theater, this never proceeds smoothly. For there are many symptoms that have to be integrated into the painting by finding the right words that will enable the child to displace a crisis.

The painter is there in front of the sheet of paper that is looking at him, and other painters alongside him can see how far he will go with it. What structures this intersubjective relation is everything that is bound up with what is seen—namely what is not there. What is not there can be "hate, insofar as destruction of the other is one pole of the very structure of the intersubjective relation. . . . If love aspires to the unfolding of the being of the other, hate wishes the opposite" (Lacan 1953–1954, pp. 277–278) and can have the effect of driving the other crazy.

What is circulating through the transferential relationships in the studio goes beyond what the children contribute. It is because the adult gets swept along, and because he cannot always master the unbearable feelings he experiences, that he has to question, as an analyst, his act of speech. From his own position, the analyst must be attentive to the fact that every transference reveals an imaginary relation that appears at certain points in the spoken encounter with the other. True speech does not preclude error, but it can slip away from revelation and take a turn toward deception (Lacan 1953–1954, p. 283). There are always gaps in the subject's story, and, Lacan emphasizes, it is what has been cast out that, later on in the intersubjective relation, will crystallize in the imagination. When the resistances emerge, the analyst will do well not to denounce them. As Octave Mannoni used to say, we don't analyze the transference; we analyze *in the field of* the transference. One has to know how to let things take their course, and not forget that, as Lacan reports the view of St. Augustine, "very often people say things that go much further than what they think, and . . . they are even capable of admitting the truth without adhering to it" (1953–1954, p. 266, translation modified).

It is with this type of analytic listening that we work in the studios. We do not take what a child says at face value, and we know how to keep negativity in abeyance and to remain sensitive to the humor, but also to the suffering, of someone who can speak only through shouting and the rebellion of his body.

Ethologists have shown that struggle on the level of the imaginary exists in the animal kingdom; in a tense situation, each animal "takes his bearings on the other's image," and both of them "avoid a real struggle which would lead to the destruction of one of them" (Lacan 1953–1954, p. 282). For human beings, on the other hand, the imaginary "is centered on the specular image." The ego appears as an ideal ego at the time of the exhilarating mirror identification, when the subject is still in a state of prematuration. From the time of the mirror stage, Lacan says, the image of the ego is still connected with "an original deficit, a gap to which it remains linked in its structure" (p. 282).

Later on, the subject will always search in the other for his own ideal ego. Here we find an aspect of the role played by the transferential object. What distinguishes the studio leader from a cop on duty is that, as an analyst, he is attentive to his own potential violence *before* addressing the child. He thus avoids committing an act of aggression that would put him in a position of dominance, a position that would draw the other into a dyadic "fight to the death" on the level of the imaginary.

"These are children without words who have been our guides. The studio was built around autistic children" (Claude Halmos, personal communication). The group began with very severe cases: some of the children, in despair, had abandoned speech entirely, while others felt that they were in mortal danger if they had to speak to someone. These children could express the terror that inhabited them only by breaking things; they had no Other stage on which to display their anxiety.

As part of the frame, a ritual was established to open and close the painting session.[6] It served as a reassuring container for the panicky fears of such children. Some painted on the ground, the paint being merely an extension of their bodies; others painted standing up; others had, in effect, no hands, since they held so many pebbles that there was no room for a paintbrush. One day we said to François, "That's because your mother puts you in her hands so that you won't have hands any more." He began to shout and to weep, and then he painted the horror that was inside him. These horrors that could not be put into words always seemed to involve unthinkable separation anxiety. When every separation is experienced as annihilation, all the child can do is construct for himself a world in which he tries hard to live without affects in order to keep himself safe from the threat of destruction. When, thanks to analysis, he loses his autistic armor, he still has far to go: having become vulnerable, he remains fascinated by death and runs the risk of suicidal acting out.

Frances Tustin (1972), following Bettelheim, emphasizes that mothers of autistic children should not be held

---

6. The words of the ritual were: "tongue cut out, eyes gouged, ears stopped up, we were going to let out the cry that brings light" (Claude Halmos, in M. Mannoni 1976, p. 112).

solely responsible for the child's problem. In some cases, we can say that it is "no one's fault," since it is the child who rejects his mother. Then autism sets in if the mother, feeling guilty because she has been rejected, turns away from the child because she feels accused of being a bad parent. The task of analysis in such cases is not to tackle the child's defenses but to elicit the truth of these defenses.

The autistic children that we initially had in our studios,[7] together with older psychotic and retarded children, were in analysis outside of Bonneuil. They could be integrated into the studios only when we gave them special attention in a "maternal" style. In other activities, such as water play, we met with them individually, our concern being to protect them from noise and aggression from without. This background of safety and discreet but effective individual accompaniment, even in the group studios, made it possible for them to take their places as artists and actors.

When such children begin to speak, it is often with derision and deception. They feel "empty," the void being

7. The number of autistic children decreased later on. The government (in 1992) did not give us funding to set up an experimental service for adults, which would have allowed families to take them in and craftspeople to give them work. The most serious cases were not able to lead a normal life, but we found them accommodations in the village, where they are able to enjoy relative independence. With the authorization we have now received, this service will enable these adults to continue a way of life at their own level and avoid psychiatric hospitalization and other forms of institutionalization.

the non-existence of symbolization and the imaginary. Visual expression enables them to give a name to the inexpressible horror. One little girl, Sandrine, existed only when she was in a state of violent crisis, throwing herself to the ground in order to hurt herself and destroying everything around her. At first the outbursts became more frequent, since the adult did not take her unhappiness into account. She got herself excluded from the studios in the name of a "ban on exploitation," a prohibition that had not been thought out analytically but was merely a reflex on the part of a junior teacher. Claude Halmos realized that she had to approach the child in a different register; she heard Sandrine's distress and found the words with which to speak of her "misfortune." She told her that it must be hard for her to be in trouble all the time, leading the big people to throw her out. The big people needed her help, since at different times they spoke a language that could not be understood and there was no interpreter.

Another child, Théophile, began to scream and throw paintbrushes one day. He calmed down when told, "You're shouting, maybe because you're scared. Bernadette is here beside you. You don't have to be scared any more." Théophile stopped screaming and began to paint.

What interests me in the way this studio developed from the beginnings of Bonneuil is that the adults were willing to learn from the child, to name his suffering and integrate it with his symptom in the activity of painting. And we sometimes had visits from real painters in this studio that, one day, was named for Vincent van Gogh, whose story was told to the children. Thus mental illness was given a place in daily life and a connection was forged to what lies beyond us.

Grotowski (1968) tells us that, for Artaud, actors must be like martyrs who try to communicate with us even as they are being burned at the stake. And, indeed, the painting of these children who had been flayed alive was signaling to us. Later on we got the idea of putting up an enormous sheet of paper from floor to ceiling and calling it the "tree of life." The children's paintings were placed on this "tree" after each session. At the end of the year, the children selected which pictures they wanted to be shown in a gallery of paintings and which were to be burned "to feed the earth."

From the analytic point of view, it was the most re-markable paintings that were destroyed in the course of a sacrificial "ceremony" in which the children danced and sang around the fire. They were hardly concerned with the pictures to be exhibited, but what *had to be* destroyed seemed crucial to them, enabling them to survive as sub-jects and not be reduced to the status of manipulated objects. This destruction represented the erasure of their shame, their fear, their fear of being labeled, yet again, as crazy.

These children, so severely stricken in their very being, were thus able to go the small distance from the place of desire alienated in the other (the place that is occupied before the advent of language and that entails the destruction of the other) to the stage at which the subject apprehends himself as "me," after which he can project his desire outside himself. From this, Lacan says, there nevertheless arises "the impossibility of all human coexistence." But, fortunately, the subject grows up in "a world of others who speak. That is why his desire is susceptible to the mediation of recognition. Without which every human function would simply exhaust itself in the unspecified wish for the destruction of the other as such" (1953–1954, p. 171).

It was thus essential for us—in the studios, in the educational program, in the entire way of life at Bonneuil—to stay attuned to a language without words. In this way we were able to integrate the crises into a true speech that spread out for the child a field in which human desire is mediated by entering the system of language (the laws governing exchange, etc.). This intersubjective relation, however, is fragile. It is not enough for the adult to speak. He also has to provide a place in his speech for a possible mediation between the subject and the other, so that he does not lapse into a violence that would suppress the other as subject.

# 8

## *Hans Christian Andersen: a Childhood, a Life*

In 1847, Hans Christian Andersen (1805–1875) completed the German edition of his work with an autobiography (English translation: Andersen 1871). Enormously successful and widely translated, the autobiography was revised and supplemented over the years, but it was in 1847 that Andersen was at the height of his international fame, surrounded by royalty and admired by poets. His youth of poverty and multiple hardships was now behind him. His autobiography was intended as a commentary on his work or an illustration of it, perhaps as the most masterful of his stories, a combination of the work and the life.

The successive translations of the original title pose a challenge to the interpreter. This life set forth originally as an "adventure" (in Danish, *Mit Livs Eventyr*, [*My*

*Life's Adventure*]) or "tale" was elsewhere presented as a "true history" or "fairy story." Moreover, the subsequent revisions involved a change in style. The storyteller's gift appears in the first English translation, which is fresh and spontaneous, while later there is an overt concern to "tell all." But it is the subject's relation to his own life that is always at work in Andersen's writing (cf. O. Mannoni 1990). This is not reportage but an investigation into how his life and his work come together into a whole.

The family romance, in the autobiography, is presented as exemplary; the most painful time of Andersen's childhood—the poverty and abandonment—is idealized, and a wave of the magic wand transforms the most somber realities into a fairy tale:

> My life is a lovely story, happy and full of incident. If, when I was a boy, and went forth into the world poor and friendless, a good fairy had met me and said, "Choose now thy own course through life, and the object for which thou wilt strive, and then, according to the development of thy mind, and as reason requires, I will guide and defend thee to its attainment," my fate could not, even then, have been directed more happily, more prudently, or better. The history of my life will say to the world what it says to me: there is a loving God, who directs all things for the best. [1871, p. 1]

When his mother died, Andersen dedicated to her memory a story entitled "She was no good" (Andersen 1985, pp. 452–458). The son of an alcoholic washerwoman meets up with the mayor, who voices his strong disapproval of the mother's behavior. The child then finds his mother standing in the water doing laundry; when she complains of the difficulty of her life, the child gives her alcohol to drink. She feels ill and is taken home, where she recounts her memories: a kindly employer who did not tell her that she was good for nothing, then marriage to a fine man. A life of ease was followed by hard times, ruin, the birth of the little boy, the death of the husband. When she recovers, the mother returns to her life as a washerwoman, but one day she slips, strikes her head on the ground, and is killed. At the same moment, the boy learns that the mayor's brother has just died and has left a bequest to the washerwoman and her son in recognition of the services they had performed for him. The mayor promises to take care of the boy, to place him with upstanding people and see that he is trained for a craft; the boy, he says, should be glad for the death of a mother who was good for nothing.

At the graveyard, the weeping child places a rose on his mother's tomb. "'My sweet mother,' the child said, with the tears running down his cheeks. 'Is it really true that she was no good?' 'Oh, she was good,' said [his friend] Maren, '. . . and God in His Heaven will say the same; let the world go on saying she was no good'" (p. 458).

Andersen's father, a cobbler, was a storyteller who read *Thousand and One Nights* to the boy and saw to it that he attended the village school. During their long walks, his father told him about history, the Bible, and the plays of Hilberg. A lover of the theater, he made a toy marionette stage for his son, and it was here that the young Andersen gave life to his daydreams, hoping one day to create plays worthy of Shakespeare. He was barely eleven years old when his beloved father, ill from the campaigns of the Napoleonic Wars, died in wretched poverty instead of the social betterment he had hoped for.

From his father, Andersen retained an early love for reading and the aspiration to escape his milieu, but his actual inheritance was misery and ignorance. Andersen's illiterate mother wanted to restrict her son to the level of local folklore, making him miss school and drawing him into her world of superstitions. An alcoholic and remarried to one, she lived in a constant state of misfortune, a pariah, in a world that Andersen wanted to escape at any cost. Cherishing the memory of the carnivals, the military parades, and the theatrical performances to which his father had taken him, he felt that he was destined to become a great actor or a famous poet. Though he dearly loved his mother, he had no hesitation in leaving her, when he was fourteen and she was lost in alcoholism, to try his luck in Copenhagen, where he presented himself at the Royal Theater.

Even though actors and singers began to take an interest in this young man, ugly, a nobody, but eager and persistent, he tried in vain to get his works publicly performed. The miracle occurred when he met Jonas Collin, a member of the board of the Royal Theater. This cultivated and kindly man became the boy's benefactor, promoting his literary work and encouraging him as an actor and singer, telling him that, frankly, he was not very good at that time but might improve if he were not too impatient. First Andersen had to learn spelling and Latin, and he obtained a scholarship that enabled him to attend secondary school. Thus, at eighteen, he sat on school benches with twelve-year-olds. Though he hated school, Andersen was diligent and completed his studies six years later.

Jonas Collin became a surrogate father for him, and his household a surrogate family. Andersen grew up among the aristocracy, receiving stipends from Frederick VI that enabled him to travel, to write, and to take the time to develop professionally. He became friendly with Dickens, Chamisso, Balzac, and Heine, and met Victor Hugo and Lamartine. In Denmark, however, his work was not well received. The difficulty of living in a world so different from that of his childhood is described in the story of "The Ugly Duckling" (Andersen 1985), who is persecuted by his fellow birds for his ugliness and oddity but then grows into a beautiful swan and finds a happiness he had never dared to hope for when he was little. Childhood memories, Freud (1901) observes, often take the form of "screen memories" that are, at the same time, similar to ancestral memories recounted in myths and legends.

Andersen offers the reader a sense of a pleasurable break with an inhuman reality. Suffering is erased, to the point where his autobiography presents him as having emerged from unhappiness to the greatest good fortune. Though he tries to stay true to his earliest recollections, his memory is selective and far from historically accurate. He does not so much give information as allude to the result of an effort at self-construction; this is why he is often unclear about the details of certain events of the past. Examining his fate, he mitigates the effects of the human tragedy by describing them as the necessary path to a better tomorrow. The desire to write is closely connected to regret for a lost, idealized childhood.

Andersen describes his birth as though he had been a spectator on the scene:

In the year 1805 there lived at Odense, in a small mean room, a young married couple who were extremely attached to each other; he was a shoemaker, scarcely twenty-two years old, a man of a richly gifted and truly poetic mind. His wife, a few years older than himself, was ignorant of life and of the world, but possessed a heart full of love. The young man had himself made his shoemaking bench and the bedstead with which he began housekeeping; this bedstead he had made out of the wooden frame which had borne only a short time before the coffin of the deceased Count Trampe, as he lay in state,

and the remnants of the black cloth on the wood-
work kept the fact still in remembrance. [1871, p. 1]

Here lay the newborn Hans Christian, according to
the autobiography. In reality, however, the place described as his birthplace was one he lived in only later.
His parents were impoverished and, it seems, had married only two months before his birth in an apparently
forced union (Greenacre 1983). The mother, eleven years
older than her husband, already had an illegitimate six-
year-old daughter, Karen Marie, whom Hans scarcely
knew as he grew up.

In his autobiography, Andersen describes his father
as a shoemaker who would have preferred to pursue his
education but had been the victim of his parents' financial ruin. For his father, then, Hans represented his own
potential: he would be someone of importance. His
mother, too, reserved a special future for him: he would
not need to beg for money, as she had to. As we have
seen, the father's death put an end to these parental
dreams and plunged Hans into poverty and unhappiness,
but, sustained by his father's predictions, he found the
strength of character to escape.

The single room that constituted Hans' "house" was
not far from a psychiatric hospital for the mentally ill
and elderly. His paternal grandfather, a manic-depressive
(Greenacre 1983), was a regular patient there. The paternal grandparents lived in a little house, the last rem-

nant of their former financial comfort, next to the hospital garden where the grandmother worked. Hans speaks warmly of this grandmother, who had to live with a mentally unstable husband. Throughout his entire childhood, Hans accompanied her to the hospital and was both frightened and fascinated by the singing of the madmen and the stories of the old women. A superstitious boy, he hardly ventured outside after nightfall. The insane grandfather made strange figurines that he gave to the peasants in exchange for supplies; children made fun of him, and Hans hid whenever he appeared, ashamed to be related to him. But years later, in 1851, he spoke in praise of difference in one of his stories, "There is a difference," where a little, ordinary plant that has been scorned by a beautiful blossoming branch is redeemed at the end: "They are different, but they are both children of beauty" (1985, p. 389).

When Andersen recalls his childhood, he speaks of mistrust of other children, even withdrawal from them, after he heard one of his companions say that he was as crazy as his grandfather. But he also speaks of his great love for the adventures experienced with adults—with his father at the theater, and with the old women he found spinning at the hospital. As a child, he took part in holiday celebrations in the prison; his maternal grandmother (scarcely mentioned in his autobiography) worked there, as did his paternal grandmother, incarcerated because she had three illegitimate children, one more than the law permitted. Karen Marie lived with this grandmother, who did not impose herself on Hans' parents. Hans called his half-sister "my mother's daughter" but otherwise ignored, or rather repressed, her existence.

The paternal grandmother's stories about the "noble" origins of the family played a role in the daydreams that Hans constructed. He relates in his autobiography how, at school, he drew the "castle" in which he would live once he became a lord, explaining that he was the child of a noble family who had been kidnapped from his parents, and saying that angels spoke to him. At other times, he wondered whether God had not deprived his parents of happiness so that he himself might have a more brilliant career. From an early age, he learned how to withdraw from an unsatisfactory reality to a more exalted life in the world of the imagination.

But years later, in Copenhagen, despite the financial support, admiration, and encouragement he received, he found himself haunted by the idea of the death of a child and a mother's sadness and wrote the stories "The Angel," "The Story of a Mother," and "The Dead Child." Here death carries children away to the angelic realm of heaven, and God gives mothers the strength to endure their bereavement. Andersen represents the loss of the loved object on an Other stage, where there appears a welcoming God who is a benevolent rescuer, a sort of mother goddess undoing the evil and the pain of separation. What is most important for him is to submit to God's will in order to counter the forces of destruction within oneself. The author, revisiting his own childhood bereavements, places himself above the situation, outside the field of play, as it were. The past remains inexplicable, but Andersen's literary imagination flourishes in this misunderstanding and, under the strong influence of the philosopher Oerstedt (cf. Chesnais 1988), develops a world view in which miracles spring forth from reality.

In this view, the harshness of reality is erased by a God who fosters the miraculous: in other words, Andersen is unconsciously encouraged to substitute the richness of the imagination for a grueling life. He embellishes whatever might be unpleasant to the reader, offering comfort, pleasure, and relief in place of ugliness and cruelty, just as he represented his own unhappy childhood as having been superseded by happiness and success.

Throughout his life, his relation to children was marked by the humiliations he experienced in his early years. He could not bear to be touched and, afraid of crowds, he preferred to read his stories before children who would sit and admire him from a distance. As Greenacre (1983) reports, he could converse pleasantly with them after he had been listened to and appreciated. But his first reflex was one of fear. A poor speaker of English, he bored a child audience in England, was heckled, and fled the room. In contrast, he recited an endless series of stories to the children of friends back in Copenhagen, fascinating them with his vivid narrative skill.

Andersen gives his stories a visual dimension. In 1969, Kjeld Heltoft, a Danish painter, published some amazing reproductions of designs Andersen had made for his marionette theater, sketches of his travels and drawings that formed the basis for his stories. These pictures help us to understand the importance for Andersen of visually representing what he put in words. It is tempting to recall, in this context, the connection made by Jean-Baptiste Pontalis (1987) between Leonardo da Vinci and Freud: "Leonardo da Vinci orients us toward what shows forth and must be seen, Sigmund Freud toward what beckons us and can only slip away" (p. 47). Words are clumsy, Freud (1910) says, and incompletely convey the meanings that painting tends to pin down.

Andersen mistrusts the collective memory that spreads pretense, preferring the immediacy, even the brutality, of a subjective vision; what interests him is the evocation of the underlying reality beneath what strikes him at the moment. And traumas are not lacking. At the age of three, he witnessed the execution of a Spanish soldier who had killed a French soldier. When he was ten, the pupils in his grammar school were given time off to watch the execution of three people convicted of murder; still haunted by the first such scene, Andersen did not attend. In the first few years of childhood, Freud (1910) tells us, patterns are set down that retain their meanings in spite of whatever later experiences we may have. The violence and misery of his childhood, and the heavy weight of what was left unsaid—the secrets of the bedchamber, the occasional prostitution of his mother before her marriage—all this was reflected in the stories that Andersen published once a year, at Christmas time. The transfigured reality is projected outside of time, since Andersen speaks to an ephemeral public for only the duration of an evening performance or a recital tour.

In the background of his arrival in the world is the question of his origins (cf. Greenacre 1983). Was he conceived in a brothel? Is his father really his father? In certain of his daydreams, Hans pictured himself being born in prison. When he went away to Copenhagen at the age of fourteen, he visited his mother's sister, the madam in a brothel, whose two adopted daughters assisted her in her profession. This aunt lived in comfort, while his mother had to content herself with pinning her hopes on a son who would, she was sure, be famous one day. While her confidence, and that of his father, helped him to overcome his early difficulties, he waged a continual battle against violence, his own and that of others. Even as an adult, admired and respected by his contemporaries, he would sometimes be overwhelmed by an inner rage that caused him to break down and sob.

Ultimately, what Andersen experienced was the primal anxiety of which Winnicott (1958) speaks. Even as a child, he had to miss school because of anxiety attacks, and, in adulthood, he was highly sensitive in his relations with others, even with his mentor, Collin. He was quick to feel wounded, rejected, insufficiently accepted and loved. The care with which his autobiography describes the accolades he won abroad—where he was treated like a hero—has its counterpart in the rejection he often, and unjustly, met with in Denmark. He recalls how, returning from one of his triumphant journeys, he overheard someone saying that he was like a performing monkey sent on tour. Though he took comfort in the high honor in which he was held elsewhere, he was nevertheless profoundly hurt.

Up to the end of his life, Andersen was tormented by instability and depression, haunted by the fear of going insane and the dread of death. In this sense he is close to Charles Dickens (an admirer of his), another writer who enjoyed fame but remained troubled by his painful childhood. Dickens writes, identifying with his characters, of sadness, hopelessness, and thoughts of death. But Dickens was married and had ten children in fifteen years. Andersen took refuge in celibacy and never owned his own house. To his last day, he sought a family that would adopt him, consider him a son. It is from the unhappiness of their lives that these two great authors created works of fiction, seeking in a constantly repeated sublimatory effort to transpose onto an Other stage the conflictual universe in which they had to live their lives. There were times when jealousy and bitterness swept over them, but in their writings comedy arises from the most dreadful situations. For each of these men, his "family romance" enabled him to escape the weight of a past to which he nonetheless kept on returning as the source of living portraits truer than reality itself.

When Dickens was a child, his father proudly seated him on a pub table to recite a popular poem. Andersen's father took him on endless walks, during which he conveyed the excitement of history and of the theater. It is surely relevant that this paternal accompaniment into the world of fiction produced great storytellers who created for their readers a transitional area between fiction and reality. Death, rage, existential distress, the burden of things left unsaid in childhood: these are the strands of which the stories are woven. As Freud tells us in his study of Leonardo (1910), even if psychoanalysis cannot fully explain the nature of artistic creation, there can be no doubt about the importance of the early years of childhood.

Elsewhere, Freud (1908a) emphasizes the correlation between creative writers' childhood memories and their literary work, which sometimes seems to be the continuation or the transposition of the close ties to one or the other parent from an early stage of life when play was in counterpoint to reality. The more painful reality is for the child, the more important is the ability of the parents to dream along with him of a different world in which the wondrous has its rightful place, its place as the inspiration for the poet and the storyteller in search of the lost language of childhood.

# *Conclusion*

Freud always asserted that writers and artists were his true masters. For him, artistic creation was another path toward knowledge of the unconscious, since the artist reveals to the analyst a truth of the unconscious that eludes him. It is for this reason that, for the past twenty years, analysts have taken an interest in picture books for children aged three to five (cf. Spitz 1988), books meant to be read *to* children, not *by* them. One of these books, *Where the Wild Things Are* (Sendak 1967), has become a classic, translated into various languages. Maurice Sendak sets the scene in a dream: this is the dramatization of a subjective state on the boundary between fantasy and reality, the creation of a transitional space between the two domains. The third party, the container for the child's anxiety, is the adult who reads a story in which the pictures are full of significance. When the image is called upon to fill in the gaps in the text, the child is tacitly invited to continue his inner voyage.

The hero of the book, a little boy named Max, disguises himself as a wolf and does so many silly things that his exasperated mother calls him "wild thing." "I'll eat you up," replies Max, who is sent to bed without dinner. We see him in his room, dressed in his wolf costume, with the window open. The forest grows right into his room and fills it completely, and then we are in the outside world and the child is sailing his boat, which is called Max, on the waves. For more than a year, he sails the ocean to the place where the wild things are and sees them dancing, roaring, gnashing their teeth, rolling their eyes, and showing their claws.

Max tames them with his magic wand, and for page after page, pictures without text show us King Max singing and dancing with the animals. Then, suddenly—and here the text returns—the child says, "Stop!" and sends them to bed without dinner. Max feels lonely. In front of his tent, he smells food and he has had enough of being the king of the wild things. He wants to be loved. Taking his wand, he sets off, but the wild things run after him, begging him not to go and saying that they love him so much, they will eat him up. "No," says Max, and the wild things begin to roar and gnash their teeth. Max says goodbye to them and sets out on his boat across the ocean. After many months, he suddenly finds himself in his room, where his dinner is waiting for him. The child is radiant with joy: nothing has changed in his room. On the final page of the book, there is no picture, just the words, "and [his dinner] was still hot."

I had the occasion to read this book to a two-and-a-half-year-old girl and was struck by the way in which the child was immediately caught up in the oral-sadistic world of the wild animals. Sometimes, when there was just a picture and no text, she would take the book and run away, patting the picture fearfully before dissolving in laughter. The child was thus taking part in a performance similar to that of Punch and Judy shows, in that a space was created in which she could get some distance from the persecutory figures of her fantasies (cf. O. Mannoni 1988).

In Sendak's story, we do not see the mother, and we hear her voice only once. The story unfolds in a familiar place that opens out onto an interior drama as the child is carried off into the world of his own fantasies. I was surprised to note that this little girl ran away with the pictures at the point where, in the story, fantasy overlaps with reality. When she came back to hear the end, to rediscover the world of words, it was like a return to an intersubjective reality connected with the presence of an adult and the adult's voice.

The dialectic between image and voice refers back to something like the family romance. Max's misdeeds—in which he takes great delight—involve fantasies of hanging a baby animal and clawing through walls, of the loss of the mother, of denial and omnipotence, of devouring. Max dominates his persecutors, protected by magic. Identifying with his mother, he threatens the animals with the same sort of punishment that she imposed on him. He then has to experience aloneness and the loss of omnipotence and rediscover the words that soothe: he learns that he and others can survive the ravages of his destructive drives. In this situation, the pages devoted to pictures without text enable the listening child to make the scenario his own by projecting his own fantasies onto it. He is given a space in which to re-create the world as he wishes, venting affect and experiencing a pleasurable relaxation of tension. The pleasure we take in reading, says Octave Mannoni (1988), comes not just from having the right to dream without guilt or shame; it also comes from being able to dominate in our reveries.

The loss of the feeling of omnipotence, which comes about through the experience of aggressivity, mobilizes the mechanisms of creation and imagination. The play space, which is also the space of analysis, is the place in which the subject questions who he is. Where there is trust and reliability, a potential space opens up, "an infinite area of separation, a space that the baby, the child, the adult can fill creatively through play; this is what will later become the successful use of the cultural heritage" (O. Mannoni 1980, p. 126).

It is our task, today, to develop this cultural heritage of psychoanalysis in all its diversity.

# References

Andersen, H. C. (1871). *The Story of My Life.* New York: Hurd and Houghton.
———— (1985). *Complete Fairy Tales and Stories of Hans Andersen*, trans. E. C. Haugaard. New York: Penguin.
Artaud, A. (1967). *Collected Works*, trans. V. Corti. New York: Calder & Boyers.
Auerhahn, N. C., and Laub, D. (1987). Play and playfulness in Holocaust survivors. In *Psychoanalytic Study of the Child* 42:45–59. New Haven, CT: Yale University Press.
Bertherat, T., and Bernstein, C. (1976). *Le corps a ses raisons.* Paris: Seuil.
Bettelheim, B. (1984). Afterword. In C. Vegh, *I Didn't Say Goodbye*, pp. 171–197. New York: Dutton.
Bleger, J. (1981). *Symbiosis y Ambiguidad.* Buenos Aires: Paidos.
Bonaparte, M. (1949). *The Life and Work of Edgar Allan Poe.* London: Imago.
Bouquier, J. J., and Richer, M. J. (1976). Le théâtre de l'inconscient. In M. Mannoni, *Un lieu pour vivre*, pp. 164–176. Paris: Seuil.

Brook, P. (1968). Preface. In J. Grotowski, *Towards a Poor Theater*, pp. 13–14. New York: Simon & Schuster.

Chesnais, P.-G. de la. (1988). Préface. In *Contes d'Andersen*, pp. 24–29. Paris: Mercure de France.

Crumb, G. (1970). *Ancient Voices of Children*. New York: C. F. Peters.

Deleuze, G. (1970). Preface. In L. Wolfson, *Le Schizo et les langues*. pp. 15–19. Paris: Gallimard.

Diop, B. (1967). *Les Contes d'Amadou Kamba*. Paris: Présence Africaine.

Dolto, F. (1981). *Au jeu du désir*. Paris: Seuil.

Dor, J. (1998). *Introduction to the Reading of Lacan. The Unconscious Structured Like a Language*, ed. J. F. Gurewich. New York: Other Press.

Eckstaedt, A. (1984). *Les Années brunes*. Paris: Confrontation.

Epstein, H. (1979). *Children of the Holocaust*. New York: Putnam.

Freud, S. (1899). Screen memories. *Standard Edition* 3:299–322.

——— (1900). The interpretation of dreams. *Standard Edition* 4/5:1–626.

——— (1901). The psychopathology of everyday life. *Standard Edition* 6:1–290.

——— (1907). Delusions and dreams in Jensen's "Gradiva." *Standard Edition* 9:1–95.

——— (1908a). Creative writers and day-dreaming. *Standard Edition* 9:141–153.

——— (1908b). Hysterical phantasies and their relation to bisexuality. *Standard Edition* 9:155–166.

——— (1909). Family romances. *Standard Edition* 9:235–241.

——— (1910). Leonardo da Vinci and a memory of his childhood. *Standard Edition* 11:57–137.

——— (1912–1913). Totem and taboo. *Standard Edition* 13:1–161.

——— (1914). On narcissism: an introduction. *Standard Edition* 14:67–102.

——— (1915). Thought for the times on war and death. *Standard Edition* 14:273–300.

———— (1916–1917). Introductory lectures on psycho-analysis. *Standard Edition* 16:241–477.

———— (1919). The "uncanny." *Standard Edition* 14:273–300.

———— (1920). Beyond the pleasure principle. *Standard Edition* 18:1–64.

———— (1925). An autobiographical study. *Standard Edition* 20:1–70.

———— (1926). Inhibitions, symptoms, and anxiety. *Standard Edition* 20:75–174.

———— (1929). Civilisation and its discontents. *Standard Edition* 21:57–145.

Green, A. (1986). *On Private Madness.* London: Hogarth.

Greenacre, P. (1983). Hans Christian Andersen and children. In *Psychoanalytic Study of the Child* 38:617–637. New Haven, CT: Yale University Press.

Grotowski, J. (1968). *Towards a Poor Theater.* New York: Simon & Schuster.

Gurewich, J. F., and Tort, M. (in press). *Lacan and the New Wave in American Psychoanalysis: The Subject and the Self.* New York: Other Press.

Hartmann, H. (1955). Notes on the theory of sublimation. In *Psychoanalytic Study of the Child* 10:9–29. New York: International Universities Press.

Heltoft, K. (1969). *Hans Christian Andersen as an Artist,* trans. R. Spink. Copenhagen: Royal Danish Ministry of Foreign Affairs and Cultural Relations.

Horowitz, M. (1976). *Stress Response Syndromes.* New York: Jason Aronson.

Khan, M. R (1983). *Hidden Selves. Between Theory and Practice in Psychoanalysis.* New York: International Universities Press.

Klein, M. (1948). *Contributions to Psycho-Analysis, 1921–1945.* London: Hogarth.

Kris, E. (1955). Neutralization and sublimation. Observations on young children. In *Psychoanalytic Study of the Child* 10:30–46. New York: International Universities Press.

Lacan, J. (1949). The mirror stage as formative of the function of the I. In J. Lacan, *Écrits. A Selection*, trans. A. Sheridan, pp. 1–7. New York: Norton, 1977.

——— (1953–1954). *The Seminar of Jacques Lacan. Book I. Freud's Papers on Technique*, ed. J.-A. Miller, trans. J. Forrester. New York: Norton, 1991.

——— (1955–1956). *The Seminar of Jacques Lacan. Book III. The Psychoses*, ed. J.-A. Miller, trans. R. Griggs. New York: Norton, 1993.

——— (1958). On a question preliminary to any possible treatment of psychosis. In J. Lacan, *Écrits. A Selection*, trans. A. Sheridan, pp. 178–225. New York: Norton, 1977.

——— (1958–1959). Le désir et son interprétation. Unpublished seminar.

——— (1959–1960). *The Seminar of Jacques Lacan. Book VII. The Ethics of Psychoanalysis*, ed. J.-A. Miller, trans. D. Porter. New York: Norton, 1992.

——— (1964). *The Four Fundamental Concepts of Psycho-Analysis*, ed. J.-A. Miller, trans. A. Sheridan. New York: Norton, 1978.

——— (1966). *Écrits*. Paris: Seuil.

Laplanche, J., and Pontalis, J.-B. (1973). *The Language of Psycho-Analysis*, trans. D. N. Smith. London: Hogarth.

——— (1985). *Fantasme originaire, fantasme des origines, origine du fantasme*. Paris: Hachette.

Lévi-Strauss, C. (1949). *The Elementary Structures of Kinship*, trans. J. H. Bell, ed. R. Needham. Boston: Beacon, 1969.

Mahler, M. S. (1963). Thoughts about development and individuation. In *Psychoanalytic Study of the Child* 18:307–324.

——— (1968). *Infantile Psychosis*. New York: International Universities Press.

Malson, L. (1972). *Wolf Children*, followed by *The Wild Boy of Aveyron*, by Jean Itard, trans. E. Fawcett, P. Ayrton, and J. White. New York: Monthly Review Press.

Mannoni, M. (1973). *Éducation impossible*. Paris: Seuil.

——— (1976). *Un lieu pour vivre*. Paris: Seuil.

———— (1979). *La Théorie comme fiction.* Paris: Seuil.

Mannoni, O. (1968). *Freud.* Paris: Seuil.

———— (1969). *Clefs pour l'imaginaire.* Paris: Seuil.

———— (1980). *Un commencement qui n'en finit pas.* Paris: Seuil.

———— (1988). *Un si vif étonnement.* Paris: Seuil.

———— (1990). Relation d'un sujet à sa propre vie. *Temps modernes* 528:57–78.

 M'Uzan, M. de. (1977). *De l'art à la mort.* Paris: Gallimard.

Pirandello, L. (1904). *The Late Mattia Pascal,* trans. A. Livingston. New York: Dutton, 1923.

Poe, E. A. (1941). *Tales of Mystery and Imagination.* New York: Heritage.

———— (1971). *Poems.* Norwalk, CT: Heritage.

Pontalis, J.-B. (1987). Preface. In S. Freud, *Un souvenir d'enfance de Léonard de Vinci,* trans. J. Altounian, pp. 3–6. Paris: Gallimard.

Rank, O. (1914). *Don Juan et le double.* Paris: PBP, 1973.

Raponda-Walker, A. (1967). *Contes gabonais.* Paris: Présence Africaine.

Reinoso, G. G. (1987). Le psychanalyste sous la terreur. *Temps modernes,* April, pp. 17–29.

Rittenberg, S., and Shaw, L. N. (1991). On fantasies of self-creation. In *Psychoanalytic Study of the Child* 46:217–236. New Haven, CT: Yale University Press.

Rosolato, G. (1969). *Essais sur le symbolique.* Paris: Gallimard.

Schreber, D. P. (1903). *Memoirs of My Nervous Illness,* trans. and ed. I. Macalpine and R. A. Hunter. Cambridge, MA: Harvard University Press, 1988.

Sendak, M. (1967). *Where the Wild Things Are.* New York: Harper & Row.

Spitz, E. H. (1987). Separation-individuation in a cycle of songs, George Crumb's *Ancient Voices of Children.* In *Psychoanalytic Study of the Child* 42:531–543. New Haven, CT: Yale University Press.

———— (1988). Picturing the child's inner world of fantasy. In *Psycho-*

*analytic Study of the Child* 43:433–448. New Haven, CT: Yale University Press.

Terr, L. C. (1979). Children of Chowchilla: a study of psychic trauma. In *Psychoanalytic Study of the Child* 34:547–624. New Haven, CT: Yale University Press.

——— (1987). Childhood trauma and the creative product. In *Psychoanalytic Study of the Child* 42:545–575. New Haven, CT: Yale University Press.

Tolstoy, L. (1872). *War and Peace*, trans. L. and A. Maude. New York: Norton, 1966.

Tustin, F. (1972). *Childhood Psychosis*. London: Hogarth.

Vegh, C. (1984). *I Didn't Say Goodbye*, trans. R. Schwartz. New York: Dutton.

Wharton, E. (1973). *The Ghost Stories of Edith Wharton*. New York: Scribners.

Winnicott, D. W. (1945). Primitive emotional development. In *Through Paediatrics to Psycho-Analysis*, pp. 145–156. New York: Basic Books, 1975.

——— (1949). Mind and its relation to the psyche-soma. In *Through Paediatrics to Psycho-Analysis*, pp. 243–254. New York: Basic Books, 1975.

——— (1951). Transitional objects and transitional phenomena. In *Playing and Reality*, pp. 1–25. New York: Basic Books.

——— (1958). *Through Paediatrics to Psycho-Analysis*. New York: Basic Books, 1975.

——— (1960). Ego distortion in terms of true and false self. In *The Maturational Processes and the Facilitating Environment*, pp. 140–152. London: Hogarth.

——— (1971). *Playing and Reality*. New York: Basic Books.

Wolfson, L. (1970). *Le Schizo et les langues*. Paris: Gallimard.

# Index

# *About the Author*

Maud Mannoni's revolutionary influence on an entire generation of child therapists, analysts, teachers, and parents in France began in 1964 with *The Backward Child and his Mother* (English translation 1972). Her original and profound explorations of the ways in which a child's distress reflects problems in the family continued with *Le Premier Rendezvous avec le Psychanalyste* (1965), *The Child, his "Illness," and the Others* (1967, English translation 1970), and many other publications. She is best known for the establishment, in 1969, of the experimental school for severely disturbed children at Bonneuil, where her unique integration of the theories of Lacan and Winnicott drew wide attention to new perspectives on the theory of child development and the practice of child psychotherapy.

Also of interest from Other Press . . .

**OTHER**